Salt of the Earth, Tracing the Global Journey of Salt

A Comprehensive History of the World's Most Essential Mineral, and Unearthing the Historical Significance of Salt in Human Civilization

Ph.D. LOLA LUMIO

© Copyright 2024 - All rights reserved.

The content contained within this book may not be reproduced, duplicated or transmitted without direct written permission from the author or the publisher.

Under no circumstances will any blame or legal responsibility be held against the publisher, or author, for any damages, reparation, or monetary loss due to the information contained within this book. Either directly or indirectly.

Legal Notice:

This book is copyright protected. This book is only for personal use. You cannot amend, distribute, sell, use, quote or paraphrase any part, or the content within this book, without the consent of the author or publisher.

Disclaimer Notice:

Please note the information contained within this document is for educational and entertainment purposes only. All effort has been executed to present accurate, up to date, and reliable, complete information. No warranties of any kind are declared or implied. Readers acknowledge that the author is not engaging in the rendering of legal, financial, medical or professional advice. The content within this book has been derived from various sources. Please consult a licensed professional before attempting any techniques outlined in this book.

By reading this document, the reader agrees that under no circumstances is the author responsible for any losses, direct or indirect, which are incurred as a result of the use of information contained within this document, including, but not limited to, — errors, omissions, or inaccuracies.

Table of Contents

Book Introduction

Salt, the unassuming yet essential mineral that has shaped civilizations, shaped empires, and even shaped the course of human history, is a tale as captivating as it is enduring. From the primordial depths of the earth to the heights of modern culinary artistry, salt has been a constant companion to humankind, its influence permeating every aspect of our existence.

In the beginning, there was the geological genesis of salt, a crystalline marvel forged from the depths of the earth's crust, where ancient seas evaporated, leaving behind a treasure trove of mineral riches. These deposits, formed over eons, would eventually become the lifeblood of entire societies, fueling a relentless pursuit for the prized commodity.

As civilizations emerged and flourished, salt became an integral part of their fabric, woven into the tapestry of daily life. The ancient Egyptians, Greeks, and Romans revered salt not only for its ability to preserve and enhance the flavor of food but also for its mystical properties, incorporating it into religious rituals and bestowing upon it symbolic significance.

Salt's impact on human history is inextricably linked to its role in food preservation and storage. In an age before modern refrigeration, salt was a guardian of sustenance, enabling communities to stockpile provisions and weather the harshest of seasons. This ability to preserve the fruits of the harvest was a game-changer, allowing settlements to thrive and expand, laying the foundations for the rise of great empires.

However, salt's value extended far beyond the realm of sustenance. Its scarcity and demand spawned a vast network of trade routes, connecting distant lands and cultures in a web of commerce and conquest. From the ancient Silk Road to the legendary spice routes of the Middle Ages, salt was the golden thread that stitched together disparate civilizations, facilitating the exchange of goods, ideas, and innovations.

As the centuries rolled by, salt became a source of contention and conflict, its taxation a lightning rod for rebellion and revolution. The Salt Wars, waged over control of this precious commodity, etched their mark on the annals of history, with entire nations rising and falling in the quest for dominance over the lucrative salt trade.

Salt's influence was not limited to the terrestrial realm; it played a pivotal role in seafaring exploration and maritime endeavors. From the preservation of provisions on long voyages to the curing of sails and ropes, salt was an indispensable companion to the intrepid explorers who charted the uncharted waters of the world.

As technology advanced, the salt industry evolved, with new production methods and refining techniques emerging to meet the ever-growing demand. The industrial revolution ushered in a new era of mass production, transforming salt from a scarce luxury to a ubiquitous household staple.

Yet, even in modern times, salt has retained its symbolic power, serving as a catalyst for social and political change. Nowhere is this more evident than in Mahatma Gandhi's legendary Salt March, a pivotal moment in India's struggle for independence from British colonial rule. By defying the oppressive salt tax, Gandhi ignited a non-violent revolution that would ultimately shake the foundations of the British Empire.

In the present day, salt's role in human civilization remains as vital as ever, though its abundance has shifted the narrative from one of scarcity to one of excess. With concerns over the health implications of excessive salt consumption, a new chapter in salt's history is unfolding, one that challenges us to strike a balance between moderation and preservation of cultural traditions.

As we delve deeper into the annals of salt's rich tapestry, we uncover a world of diverse traditions, from the ancient salt harvesting practices of the Hawaiians to the pristine flavors of Japanese sea salt, sourced from the serene waters of the Seto Inland Sea. The rugged Andes and the majestic Himalayas yield their own treasures, with mineral-rich salts that have been revered for millennia.

In the Mediterranean, the legacy of Italian sea salt continues to captivate palates, its flavors reflecting the unique terroir of the region. Across the Atlantic, the Celtic salts of Ireland and France stand as testaments to the ingenuity of ancient peoples, who harnessed the power of the tides to extract nature's bounty.

From the sun-drenched salt flats of South America to the arid deserts of Africa, where salt has been a currency and a lifeline for nomadic tribes, the global tapestry of salt unfolds in all its diversity and wonder.

Yet, amidst this profusion of cultures and traditions, one truth remains constant: salt is an essential thread woven into the fabric of human existence. It has sustained us, nourished us, and shaped the course of our collective history, leaving an indelible mark on the tapestry of civilization.

As we embark on this odyssey through the ages, tracing the global journey of salt, we bear witness to the enduring legacy of a mineral that has transcended mere sustenance to become a symbol of human resilience, ingenuity, and the indomitable spirit that has propelled our species forward, through triumph and adversity, across the vast expanse of time.

In these pages, we will unravel the tangled threads of salt's story, unearthing the historical significance of this humble yet mighty mineral, and paying homage to the myriad cultures and traditions that have woven its essence into the very fabric of human civilization.

Chapter 1

Crystalline Beginnings: The Geological Origins of Salt

The dance began billions of years ago when Earth was a newborn.

An infant planet glowed red, with volcanic eruptions dotting her surface with fiery pockmarks. Yet deep within her core, the first stirrings of an elegant mineral waltz were underway. Tiny ionic dancers—sodium and chlorine atoms—began pairing up within primordial briny pools. These intimate pas de deux would one day transform both the geology and civilization of Earth herself.

Many factors serendipitously collided in the early tumult of creation to enable salt's geological origins. The chemicals, environments, and geothermal gradients needed to concentrate saline deposits were only aligned through cosmic luck—first, an abundance of sodium chloride dissolved within the global ocean, enveloping nascent landmasses. Violent, episodic evaporation then enabled basins to become supersaturated saline solutions. Tectonic shifts forged marine isolation and desiccation, while geothermal heat flows expedited further water loss. The sheer geologic time they were gradually allowed for cyclic evaporation, flooding, and chemical precipitation to form bedded salt layers. Eventually, extensive underground salt domes, pots, and sheets were created via flow and uplift. From this chaotic geological dance, massive evaporite formations emerged across the continents. Their purity and accessibility laid the foundation for salt's future indispensability.

The earliest evaporite masses coalesced along the margins of the Tethys Ocean, a long-lost ancestor of the modern Mediterranean Sea. Around 250 million years ago, in the Permian period, this shallow epicontinental arm of the Panthalassic Ocean connected the Paleo-Tethys and Neo-Tethys basins. Following a pattern that would repeat for eons, extreme evaporation exceeded freshwater replenishment, saturating marine pools with sodium chloride crystals. Successive evaporation and flooding deposited meters of rock salt interbedded with other sediment. Continual tectonic shifts damned these basins, entombing seawater until saturation. Over time, salt layers hundreds of meters thick were buried under the Tibetan Plateau and Central Asia. Witnessing the unseen subterranean majesty of these remote salt giants requires seismic imagination. Yet their inaccessibility hindered ancient humankind's discovery and industry despite their mammoth size.

Much closer to the cradles of civilization, the mother lodes of salt arising along the Mediterranean would prove more immediately useful. Intense sunlight, surrounded by continents while restricting ocean currents, transformed the Mediterranean basin into a salt factory over 200 million years. During the Messinian Salinity Crisis, when the Strait of Gibraltar closed, three to ten million cubic kilometers of salt accumulated as the seas dramatically receded. This created thick evaporite layers that, up to 3 kilometers deep, underlying the seafloor today. Tectonic clashes later pierced massive salt deposits, forming allochthonous salt sheets and overlying weight-pressed salts into towering diapirs. This led to folded, twisted strata and salt glaciers erupting on the seafloor. Though invisible without oceanographic surveys, these hidden geological upheavals left salt deposits strewn across Mediterranean lands. From Eratosthenes' Libya to the Levantine deserts, hunks of the ocean's dried crystalline essence awaited discovery on land. Accident, erosion, and tectonics conspired to lift mundane minerals into the reach of ancient peoples, though they knew not the long geological opus underlying salt's presence.

Nor did they fathom salt's cosmological origins when they gathered their first glittering samples. The ionic tango responsible began shortly after the Big Bang birthed nuclei like sodium and chlorine. Fusing within stars, such light elements were later blasted into interstellar space by supernova explosions. These cosmic seeds then streamed into stellar nurseries like the Solar Nebula that incubated our Sun and planets. Thus, salt's component atoms arrived with the original dust bulk deliveries that built Earth itself nearly 4.6 billion years ago. After a lengthy subterranean gestation period, evaporite deposits finally presented the sodium and chlorine package humanity would exalt as sacred, fight wars over, and flavor their foods with. For those first tribal societies discovering salt, it seemed like a mysterious manna delivered straight from celestial realms. Unaware their omnipresent spice came baked into Earth's geology, ancients gazing heavenward created mythical explanations for salt's divine origins.

Not only did ancient peoples mystify salt's arrival without grasping its deep backstory, but they also had yet to deduce the hidden order underlying its surface chaos of cubes and shards. Salt crystals self-assemble as ionic sodium and chlorine dancers partner up, joining a syncopated cubic dance embodying equilibrium. Their ordered stacking lends stability despite salt's propensity to fall apart into constituent pieces. However, for millennia, early civilizations utilizing salt knew nothing of dancing ions or crystal structures. They simply enjoyed the end product—a splendid solid precipitating from liquids or crusting dry lake beds with glistening granules. Salt's crystallized architecture was an unseen marvel, though ancients across Eurasia and Africa recognized this particular rock's utility.

The earliest suspected usage links sub-Saharan salt gathering to elephant hunting circa 6000 BC, based on the proximity between salt deposits and ancient elephant bones in the Katanda region. Perhaps early hunters noticed herbivores congregating around scattered, giant salt licks deposited by interglacial dust storms. Those indulging found their mineral cravings sated and settled in, providing stationary targets for spears. Or hunters tracked elephants to inland salt-crusted lakes, lying in ambush when the giant mammals came to drink the waters. However, the connection was made, and early humans possibly began associating salt deposits with favorable hunting grounds. They may have brought salt rocks home as souvenirs or flavor enhancers, but need to understand their nutritional role. However, small deposit sizes limited the exploitation of wild salt until organized harvesting infrastructure was developed much later.

The earliest known salt production lies in Europe's Carpathian Mountains circa 6000 BC, though discovery likely trailed first utilization by many years. Early Stone Age peoples in the Balkans, Poland, and Ukraine chanced upon outcroppings of exposed halite salt. Experimentation revealed that crushing these alluring white crystals and dissolving them in water imparted a salty flavor. Submerging clean rawhide pouches filled with halite pebbles in streams also produced salty water in primitive Salt Springs. Gradually, these salt-infused waters or damp crystals got incorporated into foods via serendipity or necessity during lean times. Roasting meats or hard grains over a salt lick likely impregnated them with hints of flavor. Such workaday trials fostered dietary salt addition and culinary experimentation. Thus, incremental steps culminated in advanced salt-curing technology that launched international commodity trade in antiquity. But they were locally foraging salt-contented communities for millennia before systematic production started.

Wild salt gathering extended from the cold Carpathians to the warm Levantine desert by the 5th millennium BC as the Natufian culture flourished amidst the Fertile Crescent. These semi-nomadic ancestors of Mesopotamians trekked seasonal routes, herding gazelles and gathering wild grains to exist in the steppes when rainfall permitted crops. Roving bands likely encountered chunks of salt weathering out of marl bluffs, glittering remnants from the dried Mediterranean basin. Hacking off pieces to season their foods would supplement their meager mineral intake until settlements like Ain Mallaha stabilized. As their taste for salt grew alongside figs, pistachios, and chickpeas, brackish springs or frequent surface deposits satisfied limited demand. They crushed precious salt rocks with mallet stones and stored the sweet powder in seashells. Thus, simple procurement methods prevailed in Salt's early days.

Further east, the arid Geo-Sino Heartland cradled budding Asian civilizations amidst scattered salts from paleo-lakes and windswept deserts. Chinese villages along the Yellow River may have collected crystalline efflorescent salt from seasonal floods evaporating off silty soil. Safe from diluvial disaster upstream, Chengtoushan or Hemudu Tempian villagers harvested salt arriving at their clay-walled doorsteps. However, demand remained low for these Neolithic millet farmers around 5000 BC, a humble era preceding the domineering dynasties. Essential harvesting from sandbars or saline playas endured for those with limited needs and no extensive trade networks. But simple surface gathering was the prelude to extensive mining and production innovations in millennia ahead.

Likewise, early Andean settlements extracted salt from surface deposits 5000 years back without refining methods. Seasonal flooding of salt lakes like Maras enriched surrounding soil, continuously replenishing accessible crystals nearby. Or coastal El Paraíso villagers may have farmed solar salt like their Inca descendants, transferring seawater into clay pans for solar evaporation. They scooped up the thin crust left behind, cooking it in ceramic vessels perhaps akin to clunky modern ollas. Curation in gourd bowls or pots is followed to preserve precious minerals leached from mountain springs or the ocean. But circa 3000 BC, cuisines were still unsophisticated in the Americas, where chili peppers, beans, squash, quinoa, and salt sufficed. Though unpredictable impacts deluging the arid coast necessitated their salt not get washed away! Simple, durable structures later safeguarded solar saltworks that irrigated civilizations.

These disparate Old World and New World genesis stories shared common threads despite unfolding continents apart. Limited salt demands were met through modest harvesting from land deposits or shallow brine sources. Crude breakage, dissolving, and drying techniques extracted salt from natural occurrences without engineering interventions. Storage and preservation could have been better than the specialized vessels and facilities. Salt remained a minimal dietary supplement for average communities rather than an excellent, motivating conflict. However, foundations were laid during this formative millennium as people explored their mineral environs. Gradually, they realized the cubic crystals left behind when the water disappeared made food taste better and last longer. Across Eurasia and the Americas, cultures accumulated localized lore that anticipated salt's illustrious heritage. However, few foresaw worldwide consequences as this innocuous ionic compound insinuated itself into every civilization arising across the globe. For the next few thousand years, salt's full impact still simmered below society's surface, awaiting discovery.

Most ancient salt uses arose less from ingenuity than from accidents of geology serendipitously enabling access. Primitive peoples took advantage of natural gifts presented in their habitats. Those inhabiting sun-drenched deserts near evaporated lakes or leaching montane springs utilized ready salt availability with little effort or technology. Indeed, salt gatherers rejoiced when rains refilled their local Sawa, Sebkha, or Salinas with promising briny solutions! Reliable environmental renewal made sustainable exploitation achievable. Consumption gradually escalated through such providence from rare dietary dashes to habitual curing, trading, taxing, and territorial struggles. But at first, only minimal quantities were required for scattered tribes and villages. The actual root powering transformational phases in humanity's love affair with salts came later–ignition required the combustion engine of concentrated populations living together in cities.

The pivotal leap that changed salt's trajectory arrived circa 3500 BC when Sumerian ingenuity engineered unprecedented means for salt production. These pioneering urbanites built the world's first great cities like Ur and Uruk not through being expert geologists but rather skilled irrigationists. Summer prospered through organized agriculture and infrastructure supporting dense populations, enabling the construction of temples, walls, and surplus grain storage. The division of labor freed some citizen's time for more than subsistence activity, allowing specialization, trade, and a growing appetite for salt. Enough seasonal rainfall or flooding swelled the Persian Gulf inland, overflowing into marshes and lagoons dotting ancient Sumerian lands. But when the fierce summer sun evaporated these brackish pools, vital irrigation sources risked drying up, too, amidst the arid floodplain.

Enterprising citizens soon devised an efficient solution–excavating artificial evaporation lagoons to concentrate the brine that remained reliably after seasonal drying. Shunting lagoon seawater into a sequence of ponds facilitated incremental solar concentration into harvestable salt crystals. Channels and regulators controlled water flow rates while dikes segmented ponds, enabling easy raking and shoveling to collect white mounds glinting like gypsum. The blistering southern sun performed its most arduous duties free of charge during this elegant gravitational desalination. The Sumerians then sledgehammered massively gathered salt blocks into transportable slabs. Loading these onto boats, they sailed salt down the Persian Gulf to trade in cities like Ur, hungry for the precious mineral. Exports abroad soon followed, shipping Mesopotamian salt abroad as people acquired the taste. What began as meeting domestic demand in a land "where fish start sweating in the waters" sparked international industry and immense wealth for camel caravans dominating overland salt trade routes in antiquity.

The Sumerian saltworks marked the first known conscious effort toward scaled salt production, transforming its image from a magical divine blessing into a commercial good that was manufactured, trafficked, and taxed. Scientific foresight played no role in evaporative pond innovation–desperate necessity prompted this invention to support cities through the droughts afflicting ancient riverine civilizations. Yet necessity's offspring spawned convenience that whetted the appetites of ancients living in hot, fertile alluvial plains near salty seas. The Discovery of an indirect harvesting technique requiring only sunlight and shovels to yield piles of salt inaugurated wholesale commodity markets satisfying hunger for the flavor once limited to those near natural deposits. Currencies crystallized as money classes bankrolled production and transport across deserts and seas. Structured trade emerged from enterprising merchants ferrying slab salt for sale abroad, like their successors carrying Mediterranean murex snails harvested for prized purple dye.

The wandering Salt Life took hold on overland trails and maritime trade routes as men risked harsh travel to slake humanity's sodium thirst. Loading clumsy sailed ships required port cities like Lothal on India's northwest coast, establishing hallmarks of civilization like language, laws, and literacy to support the endeavor. Beam scales and uniform weights were developed to assess salt's value alongside silver fairly. Treatises and merchant manuals codified best practices for harvesting, transporting, and storing the dissolving crystals, safeguarding assets on multi-year business trips that one shattered container could wipe out. Salt-seeking seafarers followed favorable currents and monsoons across oceans, while cameleers traced safe paths, skirting immense desert dangers. Each embodied bold sacrifice like later spice traders, their hardship homogenizing salt access across scattered lands still unknown or hostile toward one another. Sodium commerce eroded geographic privilege as tireless salt carriers delivered the magical mineral bounty into the deep interiors of proliferating Old World empires.

The Sumerian initiative catalyzed the industry that other civilizations adapted to regional environments. The Indus Valley inheritors of maritime Mohenjo-daro built huge saltworks blending engineering and artistry around 2400 BC, evaporating brine through a sequence of high-quality kiln-fired pans visible in satellite views today. Chinese villagers harvested precious sea salt crystallizing along the boiling Zhejiang coastline as early as 2000 BC, cultivating salt farms passed down generations like ancestral lands dedicated to this exceptional shoreside crop. The Ancient Greeks dried up and dredged the fringes of Aegean lagoons beginning in 1400 BC to mine glittering white gold, ship goods abroad, and influence Mediterranean processes. West African communities evaporated brines trapped inland where Libya's arid Fezzan valleys approach the hot Sahara's margin, trading precious desert salt for forest resources like kola nuts and gold traveling opposite routes. The grand industry flowering across Ezeka, Taghaza, and Bilma later inspired fierce trans-Saharan commerce linking prosperous inland kingdoms like Mali and the forested Ashanti Empire of the Gold Coast along salt roadways.

But oceans away, the New World's complex civilizations charted more independent trajectories to salt usage despite parallel environments along the arid Andean coast, Oasisamerica home to predecessors of Southwestern tribes, Mesoamerican ancestral cities around Lake Texcoco's saltwater Alberca de San Lazaro, and their Caribbean island neighbors. Lacking the trans-continental trade exchange and idea diffusion that spread saline innovations like wildfire across Afro-Eurasia, parallel invention prevailed. Local needs mandated site-specific solutions relying on readily available resources, though volcanic glass obsidian for sharper salt harvesting tools proved a prized regional export. Tribes around the Great Salt Lake, Gran Salitral Bolivian flats, or Lake Enriquillo brine springs likely discovered saline solutions independently. They panned evaporites in pottery, dried and crushed with mortars and pestles instead of more advanced grinding wheels and presses. Nor did imperial ambitions yet drive military protection of state-operated saltworks as in China. But goods moved multi-directionally, so maritime salt still reached inland tribes via exchange networks like the Andes-to-Amazon Camino de la Sal trail. However, slaves condemned to transporting this backbreaking necessity shouldered the highest costs during the brutal rise of the New World Empires preceding European arrival.

The most notable independent invention arose from the Mayans, whose flourishing Classic Period niche economies traded household specialties. Salt makers, or yits'aak kb'ah, specialize in transforming seasonal solar salts into cake, honey, or Gruda varieties, supplying broad customer bases with a nutritionally vital good. They passed elite salt taxes up bureaucratic temple chains, ensuring wide distribution under royal oversight. Many sprawling sites, like Ek Balam near Valladolid, Mexico, likely hosted dedicated Saltmakers' plazas where brine-filled chambers evaporated under thatch roofs before firing the final solar pans. Mixing bonding additives like rice and egg whites to mineral salts created solid blocks for easy transport to inland cities along the Sacbeob road networks. Legacy techniques persist among harvesters working the Yucatán Peninsula's glittering Las Coloradas and Rio Hondo seasonal saltworks today. Yet even at its height, supplying public markets and tribute to feed millions, New World salt paled in comparison to the indispensable role played by spices in shaping global trade and culinary traditions.

Chapter 2

Ancient Civilizations Seasoned by Salt

Salt's Role in Early Agriculture and Food Preservation

Like a budding seed patiently working its way up from the nurturing soil, early civilizations sprouted along Earth's saline veins—the oceans, salt lakes, and deserts—where this precious mineral proved pivotal in transforming nomadic hunting and gathering groups into settled agricultural communities. The first farmers, emerging 10,000 to 12,000 years ago between the Tigris and Euphrates rivers near the Persian Gulf, unlocked salt's potential to preserve meat and fish. By salting excess produce, early civilizations bolstered food security against droughts or other environmental uncertainties, stockpiling surpluses to feed themselves in times of scarcity. This newfound assurance ushered in permanent villages with specialized tradespeople and artisans, complex political organizations, and grand public works projects that still leave us in awe today.

Salt shepherded nascent towns into bustling metropolitan hubs of culture and commerce. As a precious source of sodium and chloride, salt's nutritional and flavor-enhancing qualities became central to emerging culinary traditions. The earliest cookbooks from ancient Mesopotamia and Egypt used salt liberally in recipes as varied as bread, cheese, cured meats, fish sauce, and medicinal digestive aids that soothed stomach ailments. Fermenting barley to brew the first beers also required salt. Every civilization's foundation, it seems, was laid upon a bedrock of salt.

This indispensable seasoning powered early food preservation efforts, particularly curing, smoking, pickling, and fermenting meat and fish. By 2500 BCE, the Sumerians salted and dried fish like cod, herring, and tuna to provision river voyage traders. The Egyptians emulated these techniques, becoming master curers who traded their salt fish and meat through North Africa and the Levant. Salted meat even made its way into the construction of the Great Pyramids—fed to the thousands of laborers who built these impressive monuments to house the god-like pharaohs for eternity. The laborers' daily meat ration was about two pounds each, implying a massive coordinated salting-and-storage operation to avoid waste in the hot desert climate.

The Egyptians also pioneered new ways of preserving food in salt, developing a taste for pickling. Vegetables like cucumbers, cabbage, onions, and fish were packed in salt and vinegar and left to ferment in sealed earthen jars for months. This technique infused foods with tangy flavors and gave rise to a beloved pickle-making tradition still famous worldwide today. Fish processing took off as a significant Egyptian industry, with salted fish and fish byproducts fueling internal trade or being shipped abroad in amphorae containers.

By 800 BCE, the Assyrians had perfected salted fish production as a state-organized endeavor. Sardines, tuna, salmon, and other fish were meticulously cleaned, layered with salt, and pressed into barrels where fish juices were mixed with the salt to create a flavorful brine preservative. These fish were destined for royal banquets, temple rituals, and the tables of nobles, underscoring salt's enduring status symbol. Common folk relied instead on salted vegetables and barley gruels for subsistence.

Thus, from the first communities clustered around the Fertile Crescent to powerful kingdoms lining the Nile and Tigris-Euphrates rivers, innovation in food preservation profoundly impacted how civilizations arose and functioned. Salt's role in unlocking year-round food security and nutrition catalyzed humankind's transition from precarious subsistence living, freeing people to engage in politics, philosophy, arts, and leisure—laying the groundwork for all the later human progress we enjoy today.

As food preservation techniques became more advanced and sophisticated over the centuries, salt became a pillar of all major ancient civilizations' diets.

Chapter 3

Salt's Role in Food Preservation and Storage

Salt has always played a vital role in human survival and civilization. As an excellent natural preservative that helps food last longer, salt enabled groups to store hardy crops and fish that could be eaten during times of scarcity. Across the globe, civilizations used salt to overcome the problem of inconsistent food supply, providing year-round nourishment and enabling migration, movement, and conquest.

In early human groups, salt served as a simple meat preservative when rubbed into hides and animal skins. Nomadic clans traversing harsh terrain with no refrigeration relied on salt curing to prevent spoilage and waste. Tribes also used salt mines as ideal cold storage spaces for perishables. As food became more agricultural, salting remained essential—grain stores were intermixed with layers of salt that absorbed moisture. Legumes and nuts were similarly preserved via a salt coating that prevented mold and bacteria.

Fish, longtime sustenance for coastal peoples, required ample salt too—vital mineral lakes and rivers lacked. The Egyptians pioneered fish curing methods with salt-heavy brines that kept harvests edible for months. Similarly, Eastern Asian cultures relied on salmon and herring preserved in salt and rice to endure the cold months. Cured meats joined fish—pork legs, ox tongues, and mutton shoulders were rubbed with salt, smoke-dried, and set aside when the game was plentiful. The salt transformed the texture while stalling spoilage.

Cheesemaking emerged as another culinary triumph aided by salt. They curled milk with salt, creating products that avoided rapid spoilage opening new ways to store nutrients and calories. Hard cheeses lasted the entire winter. Similarly, butter is kept fresh with salting—the mineral inhibiting microbes. Yogurt, cottage cheese, and buttermilk joined the world's first fridges—cool mountain caves where salted dairy lasted for months without refrigeration.

Salted foods fueled the first long trade routes, enabling long journeys without spoilage. Egyptian saltfish reached inland towns while cured olives and cheese traveled immense distances, stalling spoilage. Salt's preservative power facilitated cultural exchange and connected early cities and empires in networks of early globalization.

By medieval times, salting's preservative prowess had been perfected and widespread. Smoked hams coated in salt could endure multi-year voyages, while salted butter became a staple ballast on ships crossing tumultuous seas. Fishing towns funded themselves solely through salt fish stocks that fed vast empires. Salt cod from the Norwegian coasts remains a timeless culinary emblem of this phenomenon.

Modern times saw salt lose its supreme status as humanity tamed refrigeration and chemicals to preserve food. Yet, it stubbornly persists in time-tested applications we still enjoy today. Its rich history reminds us of salt's enduring role in our civilization—the simple mineral that enabled mankind to overcome time and nature.

Storing Salt-Cured Foods

As civilizations advanced, sheer necessity demanded more organized and dependable methods for preserving salt-cured foods to enable consistent nourishment year-round. Storing salt fish, meats, cheese, butter, and other cured items has evolved into a science across cultures. Purpose-built cold cellar spaces were meticulously crafted to balance ideal temperature, moisture, and ventilation so salted goods lasted from harvest to harvest.

In Scandinavia, subterranean cold storage cellars were heavily insulated with thick bog moss and turf roofing to maintain a frigid, breathable environment. Sturdy oak shelves neatly arranged salt-crusted hams, wheels of cheese, and barrels of pickled fish to maximize space and order. Similar cellars beneath cottages kept dairy products fresh for months during long winters. These vital spaces required careful seasonal attention–each autumn, the cellars were vigorously scrubbed, aired out, whitewashed with lime, then meticulously restocked. Constant vigilance prevented spoilage.

Chinese peasants ingeniously repurposed waste straws as invaluable storage insulation to protect vulnerable vegetables and fruits from rot and vermin. Tightly packed sheaves lined subterranean pits holding crocks of salted foods. The mild, earthy cold, just above freezing, increased storage life substantially, while thick straw bundles stabilized conditions. As a result, staples like salted radishes, turnips, cabbages, and eggplants overwintered perfectly and were preserved for lean months.

Environmental advantages like caves or cellars were optional for successful storage, though. Native American tribes traversing the Great Plains relied on portable rawhide parfleches coated in grease and sagebrush resin. Cured venison or bison survived inside for months while tribes roamed vast terrain hunting fresh meat.

Similarly, Incan messengers relied on charqui–salted llama meat dried into hardy strips for sustenance during swift long-distance travel across extreme altitudes and climate shifts thanks to careful moisture control.

Of course, salted fish remained an essential preserved staple too, adorning tables thousands of miles inland—drying techniques like wind-curing whole cod on racks enabled Norwegian stockfish to reach Mediterranean towns intact. Elsewhere, pressed salted herrings were tightly packed in barrels, which minimized moisture and air pockets during shipping. West African traditions used rapid, extreme heat smoke-drying to craft hardy mackerel or grouper that retained rich flavor for months.

By the Colonial era, European powers had refined salted meat storage for long, cruel voyages to distant continents. Pork and beef were heavily salted using precise ratios of various grain sizes for the desired texture, then layer-packed with more salt in barricaded barrels. This dry-curing then wet storage lets ships store impressive volumes of salty protein sustenance. Infamously, the corpse of explorer John Franklin was preserved this way aboard an ill-fated Arctic voyage and stashed for years before discovery.

Today, traditions continue, albeit localized by modern technology and infrastructure. Sub-zero freezers preserve more safely, but salt curing persists culturally around foods like olives, fish sauce, sausages, and country hams. The timeless science remains as effective as ever, even if necessity has faded. Salt's unique chemistry endures, ensuring mankind always has a non-perishable lifeline during turmoil.

Chapter 4

Salt Trade Routes Enable Commerce and Conquest

Salt's Early Role as a Preservative Leads to Trade Routes

Since the dawn of civilization, salt has been one of humanity's most vital minerals. As a preservative, it enabled early communities to store food for long periods, freeing them from constant hunting and foraging. This paved the way for more complex societies to take root. During the Bronze Age, around 4500 BCE, settlements arose across Mesopotamia, Egypt, Greece, and the Indus Valley to control lucrative salt sources.

Salt's excellent preserving properties in Egypt were combined with the dry desert climate to mummify the dead. Ancient Egyptian texts reference large-scale salt production, with state monopolies controlling the mineral. Salt from Egypt's Nile Delta fueled extensive regional trade, including luxury goods exchanged for the precious crystallized seasoning. Early civilizations across Eurasia relied on salt, both for nourishment and commerce.

By 800 BCE, the Assyrians had established extensive salt trading routes across Mesopotamia. Donkey caravans journeyed for up to 40 days to collect salt slabs from desert oases, which were then exported via trade ships. Control of these black gold desert sources meant controlling the coveted mineral supply for entire empires. As donkey caravans traversed inhospitable deserts, stories arose of the 'ghost caravans ' where exhausted travelers and animals were claimed to perish, leaving only the precious salty burden behind.

In ancient India, salt mining and evaporation ponds dotted coastal regions by 2000 BCE. Urbanization arose near these saltworks, most notably the massive fortress of Dholavira in modern-day Gujarat. Home to over 50,000 inhabitants at its peak circa 1500 BCE, Dholavira derived tremendous wealth from trading salt and other goods with Mesopotamia, Oman, and distant lands. Mauryan records from 300 BCE mention organized guilds that oversaw extensive salt production and regional distribution using bullock carts and ships.

By 1000 BCE, peasants in ancient China used salt bars as a medium of exchange. The crystallized white gold was integral to early Chinese philosophy, featuring the Yin-Yang principle of opposing forces. Salt mining took off during the Han Dynasty around 200 BCE, with deep rock wells boring hundreds of feet into salt formations. As imperial Chinese civilization expanded its reach, an eastern network of trade routes ferried vital salt supplies to distant towns and cities.

The ancient Greeks relied extensively on salt from the outset. By 800 BCE, during the Archaic period, organized salt harvesting occurred near the Black Sea, Aegean Sea, and Mediterranean coasts. Athenian leader Solon mentions salaries being paid to civil servants, likely alluding to salt rations handed out. In the 5th century BCE, during the Classical period, the first treatises on food preservation and salt curing began circulating in Greece.

As Alexander's empire expanded east by 320 BCE, new territories were claimed to secure vital salt reserves. Ancient Greek traders exchanged wine, olives, and honey for precious salt from the

Crimean Peninsula, Sicily, and even distant Egypt. Massive 50-ton blocks were extracted from the vast Saharan oases, then shipped upriver along the Niger River or by camel caravan before finally crossing the scorching desert.

The ancient Etruscan and Roman civilizations began as salt societies centered around the Tiber River delta. Early Roman life revolved around the Via Salaria, an old salt route linking Rome with the Adriatic coast to secure precious imported solar-evaporated sea salt. As the Roman Empire expanded its borders, conquering territory to meet its voracious salt demands became a key driver. Entire armies marched to secure and defend lucrative salt regions like hexagonal North African salt slabs from the Sahara desert.

Ancient European peoples depended on Roman rule to supply this essential mineral. Salt production took off in Britannia by 400 CE to make salted meats, fish sauces, and cheeses for far-flung Roman territories. Celtic British tribes grew rich off 'wich houses' where they boiled seawater to make salt and traded it across occupied lands. When Rome fell in 500 CE, and the Germanic barbarian invasions disrupted salt supplies, entire communities descended into hardship.

This vital role of salt in enabling trade and riches across Bronze Age societies was pivotal. As donkey caravans and boats laden with crystalline white gold traversed continents, salt became the first global commodity and thrust humanity into a proto-globalization. Our conception of trade, commerce, and economic specialization arose from humanity's insatiable desire for the magical white crystal.

Control of Salt Resources Allows Empires to Wage War and Extract Tribute

As civilizations grew dependent on vital salt trade routes, control of salt deposits conferred immense political power. Rulers soon realized that dominating the production and distribution of this widely consumed commodity enabled them to finance wars, control subject populations, and extract tributes. The humble mineral's role in preserving meat and enabling long-distance travel made it a critical strategic resource.

Parthian and Roman armies clashed over control of the Caspian Gates mountain pass in the first century BCE. This narrow corridor connecting Central Asia to the south was a vital artery for caravans loaded with silk, spices, and salt. By dominating this geostrategic pass, ambitious rulers could tax the trade and finance their territorial ambitions. The Roman general Crassus invaded Parthian lands with over 40,000 troops in 54 BCE, hoping to capture this gateway and nearby Nisibis with its fabled salt springs and mines. At first, he extracted tributes worth millions from cowed Mesopotamian cities. Soon, the Parthian horsemen rallied and annihilated his forces using mounted archers.

The Roman Empire's stationary legions did not match Parthia's fast-moving cavalry. Crassus was captured alive, and molten gold was supposedly poured down his throat as punishment for his boundless greed. This early example showed how control over salt production allowed rulers to accumulate the wealth necessary for waging wars of conquest. It also revealed the influence of geography—with flat plains suiting Roman infantry tactics while hilly terrain favored Parthian mobility.

In medieval Europe, expensive abbeys, monasteries, and cathedrals were often financed by salt revenue and tithes. By the 8th century CE, emperor Charlemagne capitalized on salt's preservative properties to incentivize clearing forests for farming. Swathes of land were offered tax-free to settlers if they transported cargoes of salt meat to feed work crews laboring over early infrastructure projects.

Coastal salt works arose near Rennes, Aigues-Mortes, Guérande, and Noirmoutier in modern-day France to mass-produce supplies for curing pork. Rising demand led to the overharvesting precious oak woodlands to fuel brine boiling operations. As pigs feasted on fallen acorns, the introduction of salt curing enabled the preservation of ham and bacon for months. Ponds were constructed along the Atlantic coast to evaporate seawater through the blistering summer months. These dry crystalline remnants were then carved into 30 kg blocks and transported inland by barge up riverways.

In 9th century China, along the eastern Yangtze |River plain, peasant rebellions arose against crushing taxation by provincial governors. Unscrupulous administrators extorted grain, silk, tea, and salt from struggling farmers already toiling under droughts, floods, and locust swarms. Shandong villagers were forced to accept government salt monopoly currency at exorbitant exchange rates, which resulted in widespread hardship. This sparked the gathering rage that erupted in 877 CE under the charismatic Huang Chao, who directed his 'salt smugglers' rebel troops to raid weapons arsenals across the region.

The rebels stormed the eastern capital at Guangzhou, captured the salt commissioner, and held him for ransom. Huang Chao declared himself emperor of the Great Qi dynasty while denouncing the salt administration's burdensome taxes on commoners. Although his rebellion was subdued, the turmoil it unleashed contributed to the Tang dynasty's collapse. Once again, salt played an influential role in toppling regimes and catalyzing the redistribution of political power.

Another commodity intertwined with the fate of the premodern salt trade was timber, which was required to fuel production. Rising salt demand led the Chinese Northern Song dynasty to accelerate canal building using corvée labor, transporting large pine rafts southwards from Zhejiang to megacities like Kaifeng. Laborers sweated as they felled thousands of trees daily to stoke smoking salt wells over 24-hour work cycles. This intensive deforestation and cultivation process gradually led to soil erosion and the progressive desertification of former woodlands.

Italian city-states like Venice and Genoa built extensive trading empires centered around the 'white gold' flowing through ports like Pisa up the Po valley. Salt's excellent value-to-weight ratio meant fortunes could be shipped to distant markets by sending the compact bundles over the high seas. By 1269 CE, every family in Venice was legally required to purchase at least 25 pounds of government-produced salt annually. This generated tremendous wealth and conferred trade monopolies that were ruthlessly defended against rival cities and ambitious nobles eyeing salt tracts.

Wars broke out repeatedly as armies sacked warehouses and seized salt convoys, crisscrossing kingdoms to safeguard supplies during meager winters. Controlling salt stockpiles meant controlling citizens' access to preserved foods during the fallow months. As far north as Sweden, soldiers were partially compensated with salt, which made it a critical strategic resource that led to struggles between monarchies aiming to corner market share. Salt taxes along Hanseatic trade routes brought German merchants and states into conflict as they struggled to dominate Baltic sugar trading.

In West Africa, vast Saharan rock salt deposits were a major commodity that fueled trade between North African Berber middlemen and Sudanese tribes like the Tuareg, Wolof, and Hausa. Exchanging precious metal and slaves for camel loads of desert salt, sprawling Niger River settlements like Tombouctou and Gao acted as hubs where salt cakes were traded for consumer goods or gold nuggets from Bambuk mines that made their way into Portuguese hands after 1500 CE.

The discovery of massive salt springs across Central Africa was excitedly noted by Arab explorers searching for the mythical 'River of Gold.' Some salt resources, like Idjil wells in the Aïr Massif region, were jealously guarded secrets, enabling nomadic tribes to extract tributes from neighboring agriculturalists desperately needing salt to absorb crop nutrition and augment diets. West African kingdoms like Mali, Songhai, and Ghana rose to prominence by controlling commercial corridors where salt and treasured commodities flowed between forests and sand seas.

Further south on the continent, Great Zimbabwe's wealth and monumental architecture were linked to production from inland saltpans, which allowed the preservation of hunted game and surpluses grown from sophisticated irrigation networks. Salt was an everyday necessity and a luxury good made more precious than gold among Bantu tribes dominating regional trade. Cowrie shells imported from the Indian Ocean and exchanged for salt facilitated the rise of a prosperous merchant class in cities like Mapungubwe, Khami, and Zimbabwe throughout medieval times.

This nitrogenous mineral formed critical connective tissue binding agricultural hinterlands to commercial towns and inland resource areas to maritime trade networks across civilizations worldwide. Salt's portability, value density, and indispensability for human activity established it as a geostrategic commodity over which wars were fought and kingdoms conquered. Salt played a surprisingly influential role in birthing modern political economies by greasing the wheels of progress. If we pay attention, perhaps even the lowly salt shaker on summer barbeques still has lessons to teach about satiating universal human appetites.

Chapter 5

Salt Taxation Through the Ages: A Contentious History

Salt, the simplest and most vital of seasonings, has carried great economic and political weight across civilizations old and new. Its production, trade, and taxation tell a tumultuous story spanning millennia. The word "salary" emerges from the Latin for salt, salarium, given how Roman soldiers were sometimes paid in salt rations. Even Mahatma Gandhi staged his famed Salt March to protest British salt taxes as an oppressive monopoly. Behind such symbolism lies a complex history intertwining salt with state revenues and public unrest.

The taxable nature of salt stems from both its universal culinary and preservative uses, as well as the concentrated, government-regulated sites of its production like salt mines or evaporation ponds. Ancient Chinese texts show salt taxes were already in place circa 800 B.C.E. during the Zhou Dynasty. As the overseers of salt distribution, early rulers profited by pricing salt beyond its production costs. The philosopher Mozi, the founder of the ethical Mohist school, condemned overly high salt taxes as burdensome to ordinary people.

In parts of Africa like the Songhai Empire spanning the 14th-16th centuries, salt slabs served as money and provided up to 80% of state revenues through vigorous trade. Camel caravans would transport and sell salt across Savannah trade routes. The precious mineral flowed from the Sahara desert to bustling cities like Timbuktu, where government officials exacted taxes on salt goods entering local markets.

Similarly, as land travel improved during the Middle Ages in Europe, coastal salt production and overland trade spread economic benefits far from ocean access points. The "gabelle" salt tax generated enormous sums and popular resentment at state meddling in local salt distribution in France. The crown set up granaries in towns like Grenoble, exerting a royal salt monopoly that clashed with medieval notions of free trade. Peasant "salt smugglers" illegally transported salt on back roads to avoid the gabelle tax, risking imprisonment or death if caught.

In ethical opposition, St. Bernardino of Siena preached in the early 1400s against excess state interference in salt revenue matters at the expense of citizens. Yet the fundamental government need for salt tax income remained. Rulers spent huge sums waging wars, constructing lavish palaces, and funding exploration fleets. Salt taxes conveniently fill treasury coffers through an essential staple. By the 17th century, the French gabelle alone accounted for over one-third of state income. Resentment simmered nonetheless.

Backlash and Reform Against Salt Taxes

As salt taxes swelled the coffers of rulers across Europe and Asia, the onerous burden on ordinary citizens sparked unrest. By the 18th century, calls for reform reached a boiling point in France, where the gabelle had been levied for 500 years. Salt smuggling to circumvent the tax soared, bleeding revenues from royal granaries even as imprisonment or death awaited those seized transporting contraband salt.

With the gabelle raising nearly 150 million livres annually by the 1780s, the injustice of a regressive tax upon a basic necessity could no longer be tolerated. The cracks in France's Ancien Régime were cleaving apart. Leading thinkers like Jacques Turgot, an economic adviser under Louis XVI, condemned the costs and inefficiencies of the gabelle monopoly. Yet entrenched special interests tied to the system blocked reforms. Only with the French Revolution's sweeping changes did the National Constituent Assembly finally abolish the hated gabelle in 1790.

However, the post-revolutionary government still required salt revenues and soon imposed new taxes almost as controversial as the gabelle. Following Napoléon's rise, the French Empire's "droits réunis" reinstated state management of salt distribution, angering citizens and merchants. Yet the thirst for income persisted. Having witnessed the French turmoil, many European states chose reform over resistance. Prussia instituted a uniform national salt tax under Frederick the Great. His enlightened yet authoritarian approach spread the tax burden while blocking local smuggling and stabilizing revenues.

In the 19th century, calls again arose for open competition and a private salt trade freed from European state structures. Economic liberalization took root, if haltingly. Taxation continued evolving from palace-centered monopolies to means testing public willingness to pay. In 1823, New British taxes on salt were scaled back after outcries over their effects on the poor. Such sentiments also eased the salt tax burden across Scandinavia in subsequent decades. Yet backing away from salt taxes challenged the spending habits of modernizing states.

In Russia, the crown's vodka monopoly limited private salt distribution, which could be used to produce vodka without illegal taxation. Despite sporadic unrest, the Czarist grip on salt held firm up to World War I. Empires from the Ottomans to the Qing also maneuvered cautiously around reforming salt taxes that could curb imperial reach while cutting income. By contrast, the independent United States saw relatively few domestic salt taxes, relying more on customs levies from imported salt until the Civil War. Salt taxation thus continued to stir political tensions between the governed and the governing in the modern era.

Even amid liberalization, salt taxes remained everywhere– if less overtly than before. The search for public revenue gave this crystalline commodity an outsized role in taxation history. Yet a mutable human narrative of power, money, and rights grew around salt's immutable chemical necessity, transforming down the centuries. As governments still levy salt taxes or surcharges today on items like restaurant bills, the piquant pinch of history retains its savor long after ancient salt monopolies dissolved.

Chapter 6

Seafaring and Salt: Essential for Exploration

Salted Sustenance For High Seas

Salt's most significant contribution to seafaring history lies in its incredible ability to preserve food for long stretches. By drawing moisture out of meat and fish through osmotic pressure, salt inhibits the growth of spoilage-causing bacteria. For vessels traversing vast oceans far from land, carrying supplies of meat, fish, butter, cheese, and vegetables packed in salt meant the difference between survival and starvation.

As early Polynesian explorers traversed the seas in canoes, seeking new isles across hundreds of miles, they subsisted on fish and meats cured with solar salt from shallow tidal pools. Dried fish packed in sea salt sustained Viking raiders on long voyages across the northern Atlantic in their iconic longships. On pre-modern ships lacking refrigeration, hauling live animals for fresh meat over months was impractical, making salted offerings necessary from Vasco de Gama rounding the Cape of Good Hope to the Spanish flotillas first reaching the Americas. Armadas, setting forth into the unknown with holds full of salted cod, pork, and biscuits, endured storms, scurvy, and hostilities to further imperial ambitions.

To this day, salt cod—bacalhau—stands as Portugal's national dish. It reflects the seminal role ocean fish preserved in sea salt played in its former mastery over navigation and trade networks spanning continents. The Royal Navy under Francis Drake and Walter Raleigh defeated the once-invincible Spanish Armada in clashes, deciding supremacy over New World riches. The British seamen relied on salt pork rations for sustenance through extended naval blockades and campaigns far from the British Isles. From Christopher Columbus' transatlantic journeys to Captain Cook's epic Pacific odysseys, the purse seine hauling tons of salted fish aboard vessels under full sail powered the Age of Discovery.

Without salt's unique preservative qualities, ship captains could scarcely have ventured beyond sight of land for fear of food spoilage and the subsequent loss of ships and crews. Loading holds with salt-cured foods allowed extended deep-sea sailing, enabling bolder voyages of exploration and sustained colonial ambitions. The very contours of the modern world—from once separate societies coming into sustained contact to the formation of New World cultures through the mass migration of Old World settlers—emerged in no small part thanks to salt. Salt's capacity to enable men to go ever further without fear of starvation. While scurvy outbreaks frequently ravaged shipboard crews subsisting solely on salt cod and biscuits, such non-perishable anti-scorbutic allowed ships to attempt ambitious global circumnavigations when supplemented by limited fresh foods at stopovers. With the right victualing strategies combining salted staples and perishable fruits and vegetables at strategic ports, captains could sail unknown seas without concerns about feeding hundreds of men for years.

Thus, at a pivotal stage of human development, salt bridged the gap between populations separated by oceans, serving both peaceful trade and violent conquest. Salt profoundly shaped the emergent linkages between societies across vast distances by feeding the armadas of explorers, discoverers, invaders, and colonists. From

Ming China's epic treasure fleets traversing Indian Ocean trade winds to spice-laden Portuguese carracks rounding the Cape back to Lisbon, salt-preserved foods fueled humankind's first forays into genuine global connectivity. For the precursors sailing off, representing distant crowns, salt's invisible hand steadied unstable ships on storm-wracked seas, allowing history's most intrepid mariners to etch ambitious routes across uncharted waters.

Salting the Seas for Commercial Gain

Merchant vessels laden with spices, textiles, ceramics, and precious metals likewise relied extensively on salt as they traversed maritime trade networks for profit. Dried salted fish served as a high-protein diet, sustaining hardworking crews through storms and doldrums on lengthy East India men's routes. More importantly, salt enabled the transport and trade of perishable commodities over vast distances for the first time.

Carried below decks in the holds of lumbering, sail-dependent cargo ships, salted meat, and fish, butter, and cheese turned handsome profits when sold abroad where such goods remained scarce luxuries. The Hanseatic League dominating Baltic and North Sea trade grew rich, supplying salted herring, cod, haddock, and mackerel to inland European markets where religious strictures mandated fish consumption on "meatless days." As packet ships began crisscrossing the Atlantic on regular schedules, salt opened opportunities for enterprising New England merchants. They supplied West Indian sugar plantations with barrels of salted northern fish to sustain hundreds of thousands of slaves and overseers laboring in the cane fields.

In exchange, molasses and rum distilled from Caribbean sugar cane made fortunes for colonial Bostonian and Salem traders. By reducing transportation costs and enabling durable storage, salt thus laid the foundations for some of history's most storied trading empires that funneled Eastern luxuries to emerging Western metropolises. Cowry shells from the Maldives, pepper and cinnamon from India, and "gray gold" Chinese tea all traveled atop maritime routes plied by ships reliant on salt for victualing from East Africa to Southeast Asia.

Insatiable demand overseas for salazón—salt-cured tuna from Almadraba tuna traps– enriched once-marginal Andalusian coastal towns, funding splendid architecture still seen in Cadiz, Seville, and Huelva. As the United States expanded westward in the 1800s, salted buffalo tongues earned Native American hunters hard currency for coveted manufactured goods from far-flung factories back East. The great Pacific saluboneta break bulk workhorses hauling immense quantities of salted fish from Alaska's prolific fisheries to insatiate markets in the Catholic Philippines and the ports of Imperial China came to epitomize the capitalization of salt's age-old food preservation prowess meeting modern transportation scale.

From shipping firms reaping fortunes trading salted cod across the Atlantic to present-day sailors trafficking narcotics through the Panama Canal to lucrative North American markets, salt has served as the hidden hand enabling mercantile ambitions. While military men couched exploration in patriotic glory, profit has clung to the coattails of their risky seafaring ventures–profit derived from salt unlocking food transport and sale over otherwise prohibiting distances. Over centuries of maritime shipping undergirding global business, fortunes small and large have been made by capitalizing on salt's singular capacity to turn perishable commodities into durable, tradable goods. The very first glimpses of today's intricately

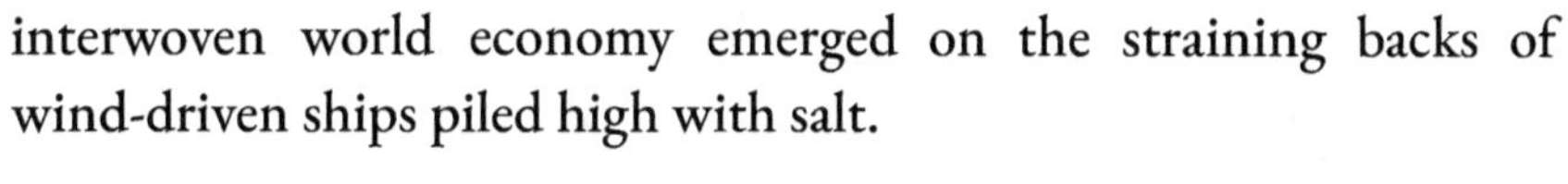

interwoven world economy emerged on the straining backs of wind-driven ships piled high with salt.

Chapter 7

Salt Production Methods Over the Millennia

Salt may be the only rock we eat, yet producing this simple mineral in usable form has challenged human ingenuity for millennia. While salt is ubiquitous across the planet, not all sources are equal regarding accessibility, purity, or the effort required to harvest it. The availability of local salt deposits and fuel sources largely dictated techniques adopted regionally over time—from solar evaporation near coastal areas to mining and brine boiling around inland surface or underground salt deposits.

Among the earliest and most straightforward means of obtaining salt, solar evaporation leverages natural cycles to concentrate seawater or other saline sources into mineral deposits ready for harvest. Practiced since at least 6000 BCE around Egypt's Nile Delta, shallow pools filled from the Mediterranean gradually reduced through evaporation, leaving crystallized sea salt deposits to shovel or rake manually at season's end. Similar solar saltworks flourished globally where water sources enabled the process: from Bronze Age China's Sichuan basin inland to Iron Age Judea's desert to arid coastal strips of India, Mexico, and Peru. Employing increasingly large, elaborate networks of artificial evaporation ponds, people pumped or channeled briny waters inland from oceans or mineral springs until achieving suitable saturation for diversion into crystallizer beds, delivering higher purity yields over time.

Where solar sources proved unavailable or insufficient to meet demand, ancient peoples extracted salt from mineral-rich soils and sand through brine-boiling. Crystalline salt deposits were leached from surface soils by soaking in water to create concentrated brines, then filtered and transferred into pots or furnaces to drive off remaining moisture through boiling, leaving behind dry salt for collection. Wood and peat from regional forests typically provided the enormous fuel requirements for heating brines across western Asia and Europe. By 400 BCE, iron cauldrons had made salt-boiling more efficient. This allowed Celtic and Teutonic tribes dwelling near Austria's alpine salt region at Hallstatt to develop advanced boiling techniques that fueled a thriving inter-regional trade network—the beginnings of ancient inland commerce in continental Europe.

Deep underground, massive formations of incredibly pure rock salt also fueled millennia of production globally—through mining. The oldest known mine for any resource, a Neolithic salt mine discovered in Azerbaijan's Chehrabad dated to 5000 BCE, marks an early milestone. China, known for pioneering technological innovations, led the world in deep rock salt mining, with shafts sunk to depths exceeding 1000 meters to reach remote deposits in Sichuan and Yunnan using bamboo scaffolding by 1000 BCE. Employing fire-setting techniques learned from Chinese immigrants, Europeans exploited rich domestic salt deposits found near alpine corridors, fueling competition among mineral-rich principalities in medieval Switzerland and Austria to gain control of the precious "white gold" output moving overland.

Salt mining and refining technology enabled quantum leaps in production but required significant capital investments. As government authorities and businessmen bankrolled ever more extensive mining and refining operations, they sought returns by treating salt less as a necessity than a revenue commodity—complete with speculation, monopolies, and conflict over routes and prices.

Salt taxes notoriously stoked tensions across regimes, from Imperial China to Bourbon France to Colonial British India. Where once pre-industrial villages shared common resources like forest fuel and brine springs, traditional access and local cooperation gave way to centralized state control and repression as salt became a cash cow milked through crushing taxes.

Fossil fuel-powered technology, vacuum pans, and mining innovations since the 1800s have exponentially boosted yields while heavily concentrating ownership in a global industry worth over $17 billion. Yet as output soared, small solar sites faded economically, just as up to 60% of the world's population relied historically on local solar or artisanal salt harvesting for their supply. Traditional saltworks from the Reddings in Massachusetts to Læsø island off Denmark became heritage tourist attractions rather than viable competitors, struggling to revive using niche production. At the same time, massive mining firms meet mainstream demand. However, some artisanal methods have persisted over centuries within specific cultural traditions where history and distinctive flavors imbue them with added value. Examples include Japan's sun-dried sea salt using age-old techniques or hand-harvested famed fleur de sel of France's Guérande region preserved through local cooperatives.

Meanwhile, salt processing diversified far beyond food applications with the advent of industrial chemistry. Thermal, solar, and membrane technologies now enable customized manufacturing of hundreds of salts with specialized qualities tailored to specific industries, from tanning hides to melting snow—even supplying caustic soda vital to manufacturing plastics and aspirin. Once laboriously boiled or raked by hand through millennia, modern salt flows from mighty mines and factories that employ the era's most cutting-edge technology to serve ever-evolving uses. Its core functions of flavoring, preserving food, and generating profits maintain continuity with the past.

Developing salt production methods may shift again as water shortages, climate change impacts, pollution concerns, or simply rising demand for gourmet varieties drive innovations from the artisanal and technological realms. Yet whatever processes come next to expand output or improve sustainability, they will remain grounded in the long lineage of salt harvesting worldwide. Salt harvesting is an ancient yet evolving nexus of geology, technology, economics, and politics as seemingly fundamental as this crystalline compound.

Chapter 8

Salt Wars and Independence Movements

Salt, the simplest and most vital of seasonings, has instigated unrest and fueled independence movements throughout history. Rulers have long recognized that controlling salt equates to managing people and economies. Consequently, the imposition of salt taxes, monopolies, and restrictive laws ignited boiling resentment that overflowed into open rebellion against oppressive regimes.

The Chinese were the first to discover that salt, essential to human survival, could be easily taxed and exploited as a revenue source. During the Qin Dynasty in 221 BCE, imperial ministers implemented the yan-liang tax on salt and iron production. The measure helped fund massive infrastructure projects like the Great Wall and stimulated popular discontent under Qin Shi Huang's draconian rule. This first "salt tax" established an unpopular yet tempting fiscal instrument that despots worldwide later adopted and enforced ruthlessly.

In France, titled nobles and clergy were traditionally exempt from salt duties under a crucial privilege called "franc-salé." But in the 14th century, the crown began imposing salt taxes like the unpopular gabelle on commoners only, fueling peasant outrage at the injustice. The universal ire sparked the Pouacre Revolt in 1636, a violent uprising demanding relief from mounting salt levies. Though swiftly suppressed, the immense hatred of the gabelle endured, stoking the fury that exploded in the French Revolution. That seismic upheaval began in 1789 when restless mobs stormed the Bastille to secure arms they would deploy against tyrannical salt agents and customs posts. Salt taxes inflamed deep passions that even the abolished monarchy and emancipatory dawn of liberté, egalité, and fraternité could not quickly pacify.

Similarly, the great Mahatma Gandhi pioneered satyagraha, or nonviolent civil disobedience, against British salt policies that devastated ordinary Indians. Since Mughal times, the ethnic Sindhi community has skillfully produced salt near coastal reservations granted by the authorities. However the East India Company rapidly disrupted traditional production from the late 18th century by boosting salt imports and exports to reap higher revenues. By the 19th century, the Company effectively monopolized the bountiful salt industries in Western India while heavily taxing salt for maximum profit.

When the Crown directly took control after the 1857 rebellion, it retained the rigorous salt monopoly despite recurrent famines that increased dependence on it. However, the prohibitively high salt tax meant most poor Indians struggled to access enough salt, forcing reliance on expensive imports. An 1882 Madras Salt Act banned Indians from accessing natural salt deposits, criminalizing all local collection.

By 1930, Mahatma Gandhi masterfully identified this unjust, undemocratic British monopoly on vital salt as the most inflammatory, tangible focus for peaceful mass protest. On March 12, 1930, Gandhi strode toward the Gujarati coast at Dandi to illegally produce salt from seawater alongside thousands of followers. This momentous Salt March sparked outrage and nonviolent civil disobedience across India until independence finally dawned in 1947. As salt taxation stoked revolution in France, oppressive policies weaponizing salt resulted in rebellion and emancipation for the world's largest democracy.

In China, the 1911 Xinhai Revolution, led by Sun Yat-sen, succeeded in overthrowing another salt-levying imperial dynasty, the Qing, after anti-Manchu rebellions steadily eroded control. The Qing had previously crushed the mid-19th-century Taiping Rebellion, a seismic uprising that killed over 20 million people, in part fueled by intense hatred of salt monopoly policies.

Later, in 1949, the Chinese Communist Party under Mao Zedong finally abolished salt taxes altogether to gain popular peasant support, just as French reformists centuries earlier had eased salt duties to appease riotous crowds during the volatile Revolution. Of course, Mao soon imposed disastrous salt policies again during the Great Leap Forward from 1958 to 1962 by mandating ammonium chloride salt substitutes. This scheme epitomized the dreadful agricultural collectivization policies that resulted in one of history's deadliest famines, with over 30 million deaths. Though the salt monopoly lay shattered, chemicals contaminated future generations, even in a supposed workers' utopia. Life-giving salt again sustained dystopian nightmares rather than uplifting dreams.

In British India, Mahatma Gandhi's unprecedented Salt March in 1930, which catalyzed mass civil disobedience for independence, also deeply inspired Nelson Mandela and other anti-apartheid activists in South Africa. After white minority rule began in 1948, Mandela's African National Congress (ANC) and allied groups opposed myriad unfair salt restrictions on indigenous workers. These included punishing salt rationing and prohibiting local salt trading, severely affecting remote townships. Embracing Gandhian ideology, Mandela led the pivotal 1952 Defiance Campaign against many unjust laws, including salt policies. This mass protest turned the ANC into a formidable national resistance organization and Mandela into a revered champion for liberty. Though imprisoned from 1962-1990, Mandela triumphed morally over crushing salt racism and emerged to redeem South Africa through peace and reconciliation.

In America, desperate revolutionaries dumped 46 tons of British salt into Boston Harbor in 1773 in what became notoriously known as the Boston Tea Party. Colonists intensely opposed burdensome taxes that invidious British laws like the 1764 Sugar Act and Townshend Acts imposed on essentials like salt. Such inflammatory duties fueled ideological outrage and discussions of independence, culminating in war from 1775-1783. The United States was born in part out of salt taxation without representation. However, native lands and lives were ruthlessly salted later for conquest under Manifest Destiny from Shining Sea to Shining Sea.

In India, Mahatma Gandhi's Salt March strategically picked up pure salt crystals from the Arabian Sea shores at Dandi, matching Columbus' 1498 arrival in the Americas discovery. Gandhi symbolized peaceful conquest over injustice without bloodshed in India's long, nonviolent war for swaraj, or Self-Rule. His scooping salt from the seas surrounding and sustaining India poignantly mirrored earlier Caribbean natives greeting Columbus with salt and water according to regional custom. Ironically, this native ritual of hearty welcome and good faith facilitated ruthless genocide and slavery for greedy gold and spice hunters soon after in the name of the salty Atlantic Ocean itself—just as the Indian Ocean had passively witnessed foreign subjugation and plunder wash up upon bendy yet strong Bharat Mata's sands for centuries before Gandhi's sweet-salty triumph.

The 1978 Salt March in Alma-Ata prefigured growing dissent against Moscow's domination of Kazakhstan. Though quashed by police, the protest helped crystallize Kazakh national identity against Soviet Russification policies, including around mining and extractive industries that contaminated fertile lands. The protest reflected Baltic outrage against chronic environmental abuses and helped galvanize similar future dissent against autocratic regimes through enduring civil resistance and disobedience tactics. Russia maintained punishing salt policies and secret cities associated with extensive Siberian mining, driving public anger in the outlying republics straining for greater autonomy and rights.

Salt, so simple yet essential, runs like restless waves through the above uprisings, carrying cries for emancipation against exploitation to the very steps of power. Too often, unjust laws weaponized the salty seasoning to inflict cruelty upon humanity, peppered with sporadic resistance unconsciously. Yet the dish can turn divine through nonviolent tactics, pairing the patience of water that carves stone with the taste-enhancing properties of salt itself. Under the surface of repression boiling with bubbling discontent, peaceful change can gently emerge through time, as when ancient seas concentrated mighty mountains into ground grains.

Salt Smuggling Fuels Black Markets and Rebellion

Wherever authorities have imposed salt taxes or monopolies, ingenious smugglers have defied restrictions through shadowy underground networks, reaping illicit fortunes. By providing tax-free salt, smugglers gained widespread support among the oppressed, salt-starved masses. Though reviled by rulers, admired smugglers became folk heroes for resisting tyranny alongside the enduring human instinct to outfox unfair systems and unjust laws.

In China, salt smuggling plagued imperial dynasties and republican regimes alike for centuries. During the Han Dynasty, around 117 BCE, politician Sang Hongyang imposed state control over salt and iron production. However, cunning merchants illegally transported salt from state-controlled areas into more profitable private markets, defying imperial salt agents. As governments successively tightened restrictions, smuggling surged, financing shadowy brokers and underground groups.

Within corrupt imperial China, struggling peasants admired legendary bandit rebel leaders like Song Jiang, who robbed salt convoys and redistributed the precious mineral to the poor as an early form of wealth redistribution. Such grassroots Robin Hood-esque figures embodied deep frustration against oppressive salt taxes that enriched faraway capitals but immiserated local communities.

When the Qing dynasty (1644-1912) established tighter frontier controls in the 18th century, many Han Chinese settlers smuggled Central Asian salt to survive in harsh environments. Anti-Qing rebels and bandits flourished by targeting official salt transports to help fund simmering rebellions. Though Beijing viewed these subversive activities as treasonous, they won loyal followers among the severely repressed.

During Republican China in the 1930s, Yan Xishan, the authoritarian warlord governing Shanxi province, controlled the lucrative smuggling routes to Shaanxi province as Shanxi lacked enough salt reserves. Yan's forces brutally suppressed independent smugglers to retain their profitable monopoly but also provided warriors to fight the Japanese invasion, exposing complex realities. Desperate peasants facing starvation pragmatically accepted any force that kept vital salt flowing, licit or illicit.

In British India, indigenous salt smuggling originated millennia ago but assumed mass dimensions after the Raj systematically destroyed traditional salt producers to establish its salt monopoly. Through brutal indentured servitude, it had become one of the world's largest salt manufacturing industries by the late 19th century. Even as monopoly salt prices plunged, most Indians could not afford heavily taxed supplies, feeding dependence on smuggled salt from local arid salt marshes (Rann of Kutch) and southern coastal saltpans, exacerbating unsustainably cash-strapped local economies.

Resented salt agents often spied for British intelligence alongside reviled tax collectors, further inflaming outrage against unjust monopoly policies. Local salt workers driven into smuggling networks frequently experienced brutal police crackdowns, with leaders facing long imprisonments and impoverishment alongside family members. Such naked oppression fueled mass affinity for defiant smugglers risking their lives against a heartless regime. It also galvanized Mahatma Gandhi's 1930 Salt March, channeling this deep disaffection into strategic nonviolent independence campaigns targeting British prestige and revenues.

In France, pervasive discontent under the loathed gabelle salt tax resulted in endemic salt smuggling, even by law enforcement. In areas called rédimés, citizens bought salt at market rates, but even there, people bought cheaper, untaxed salt smuggled from exempt regions with false paperwork. Smugglers illegally transported salt primarily through strongholds in Brittany, Burgundy, the French Alps, and areas flanking Spanish Navarre, where salt smuggling became a skilled family trade passed down generations known as contrabandists. Rough highland terrain provided ideal cover for smuggling routes, evading salt tax officials to supply inland French hamlets and towns with smuggled salt from the Atlantic and Mediterranean coasts.

Though charismatic bandit figures frequently spearheaded smuggling rings, many ordinary French citizens across classes casually engaged in small-scale salt fraud as a habitual protest against state overreach. This reflected deeply rooted opposition to the salt tax, echoing grievances that exploded during the French Revolution in 1789. Post-revolutionary authorities eased but did not eliminate salt taxes, given the fortunes they generated, thereby perpetuating smuggling traditions that boosted regional identities against Parisian centralization.

In Mexico's arid north, indigenous communities have sustainably produced salt for centuries in their home areas. However, ever since Mexico won independence from Spain in 1821, successive unstable regimes continued taxing salt and retaining military control of production and distribution. By 1888, the corrupt dictator Porfirio Díaz auctioned monopoly contracts to allies, disrupting age-old local salt self-sufficiency and forcing dependence on expensive imported salt across his vast country. Desperate northern communities, therefore, secretly harvested traditional salt deposits in remote areas like the vast Pinacate plains despite frequent deadly crackdowns. The brutal 1910 Mexican Revolution that deposed Díaz channeled deep grievances against economic mismanagement alongside other land reform and inequality issues.

The above crisscrossing currents of salt smuggling and taxation birthed defiant bandits and gangsters. But they also forced everyday civilians struggling for dignity to reluctantly rely on illicit networks that plugged profound nutritional and psychological gaps within the broken barrels of blighted systems imposed by detached, deaf rulers. And when barrels overflow down mountain gulleys after endless storms or heat waves, what spills out gets swept up by swirling undercurrents barreling for revolution as the seas reclaim salt stolen from their cradling waves. Then, the horizon shifts as shimmering salt deposits emerge elsewhere, far from the ossified halls of power.

Women Warriors Resist Colonizers Through Salt
Through imposing salt taxes and monopolies, imperial overlords inadvertently spurred localized women-led resistance movements, exposing the gender and class dynamics underpinning habitual protest. Since women handled most household food processing and cooking, they felt acutely vulnerable to volatile salt supply shortages and price fluctuations within patriarchal societies. Safeguarding family health and nutrition often fell upon women's shoulders, hardening their grit against endless adversity.

Therefore, many rebel movements found stalwart recruits among victimized women willing to risk death to secure stable clandestine salt supply lines defiantly. These valiant salt heroines surfaced across the British Empire, from India to the Caribbean, passing on sustained resistance traditions to other oppressed groups worldwide as seeds scattered by storms nourished forests.

In Colonial India's arid Rann of Kutch desert salt marshes, the indigenous Agariya community had sustainably produced salt for millennia through an egalitarian structure benefiting both women and men. However, after the British Raj monopolized lucrative salt production in the mid-19th century, Agariyas exploited migrant salt workers stripped of land rights and minimum wages. Jailed in hereditary debt bondage under brutal working conditions, Agariyas led precarious lives without healthcare or nutritious food.

Sundari Bai, an Agariya woman salt worker, endured these miserable conditions but found fresh courage after listening to Mahatma Gandhi's inspiring 1930 Salt March call for emancipatory civil disobedience against unjust British salt laws. Soon after, she defiantly led over a hundred Agariya workers to harvest Dandi's tidal salt flats, openly flouting British prohibitions against criminalizing such salt collection without paying taxes. Her bold action catalyzed many women to join nonviolent civil disobedience through parallel satyagraha salt-making demonstrations across Gujarat's coast. Though Sundari Bai faced brutal beatings and jail time, she persisted as a grassroots feminist icon, resisting imperialism alongside stalwart women marchers who enthused thousands more.

The Satyagraha anti-salt tax campaigns led by Mahatma Gandhi, Sundari Bai, and indomitable women activists tangibly demonstrated that the moral high ground was India's. Their courageous example exposed the injustice underlying the massive British Raj salt exploitation that had inflamed desperate smuggling for survival, too. Thereby, they inspired enduring nonviolent protest traditions against the criminalization of marginalized groups for righteous radical reform causes worldwide.

In the Caribbean, escaped African women slaves sustained their precarious maroon mountain settlements through ingenious salt harvesting practices away from plantation surveillance. Drying and smoking saline tropical vegetation produced vital, nutritious salt for liberated families, evading bloodthirsty British patrols and fearsome bounty hunters through the 18th and 19th centuries until final emancipation.

In Jamaica's inhospitable Mosquito Mountains, defiant runaway slave women like Granny Nanny, the national heroine, and Maroon Chieftain, safeguarded food self-sufficiency against endless attacks to protect free mountain settlements through generations. They strategically occupied the valuable Colbeck Castle salt spring amidst impenetrable forests to reliably secure this essential nutrient when famine struck their communities periodically. Nanny's courageous example of leading maroons to victory later inspired the legendary Tacky's Revolt of 1760, accelerating Britain's abolition while encouraging other rebellion leaders like Haiti's heroic Toussaint Louverture.

Similarly, in Mexico's arid Bahia de los Angeles, indigenous Cucapá women fishermen faced starvation under dictator Porfirio Diaz's devastating salt monopoly and fishing restrictions from 1888 onwards as officials favored allies instead. Daring Cucapá women, therefore, secretly undertook the dangerous Cortez Crossing through the treacherous Colorado River regularly, traversing over 70 miles roundtrip on fragile rafts to harvest ancient sacred salt deposits in Arizona, facing arrest or drowning. There, they traded illegal salt, medicinal herbs, and shells with Native American communities that respected age-old Cucapá fishing traditions that sustained delicate desert ecologies and cultures despite unrelenting oppression.

The above crystallizes how women disproportionately confronted colonizers, weaponizing salt against community health for profit and power. These defiant women nourished both material and psychological resilience by creatively safeguarding localized salt sources, production traditions, and trade routes. Their timeless courage, nourishing besieged populations, and nurturing defiance under extreme duress lights hopeful beacons through the darkness of our turbulent times. When tears drop into the sea, the first taste on parched lips remains salt. The ocean always understands heartache and responds soothingly through its essence, manifested as flavor-bestowing strength, mirrored in the bravery of heroes.

Chapter 9

Salt in Religion, Rituals, and Superstition

From ancient temples to modern churches, salt has long been intertwined with religion and spirituality across faiths and geographies. Its purifying properties and ability to sanctify items led many belief systems to incorporate salt into rituals, offerings, and places of worship.

In ancient Egypt, salt was deemed sacred and offered to the gods. Ancient temples often had salt deposits within them–some sealed and untouched for centuries. The mineral held protective powers and was used as a symbol of divine blessing and abundance by Egyptian priests. Covenants and oaths were often sealed with salt, as Egyptians believed its purity ensured commitments would be kept.

Similarly, in ancient Greece, salt was revered for its cleansing attributes. Greek worshippers brought salt cakes made of wheat, honey, and salt to be offered to the gods. Athenian children had a special bread and salt feast dedicated to Artemis each year. The mineral is also featured in holy water containers at temple entrances for purification rites before prayers.

For Jews, salt signified permanence and was customary at meals, including the Sabbath, where it represented their eternal covenant with God. During feasts like Passover, dipping food in salt water symbolically connected them to the tears and hardship of Hebrew slaves. In Judaic traditions today, bread and salt are still shared to welcome mourners back to everyday life after a funeral or period of grieving.

Early Christians used salt as a metaphor for spiritual wisdom and righteousness, referencing "the salt of the earth." In Catholic mass, a small taste of blessed salt is given to catechumens before baptism to show spiritual cleansing. The mineral is mixed with holy water to this day for blessings and consecrations in churches across denominations.

The word "salary" originates from the Latin "salarium"--the money Roman soldiers received to buy salt. This demonstrates the value placed on the mineral in Ancient Rome, which featured prominently in religious ceremonies. Priests called Salii carried out rituals involving dancing, chanting, and sacrifices, including salted flour. Breads and wafers salted with blessed salt continue to represent the body of Christ in today's communion sacraments.

Across faiths like Islam, Hinduism, and Buddhism, salt performs roles from gracing marriage ceremonies to symbolizing hospitality towards strangers. The crystalline mineral hence shares a sacred space in humanity's spiritual history, where its purity and permanence have endowed it with many layers of meaning since ancient times.

Across numerous faiths and geographies, salt has maintained a prevalent connection with spirituality due to its ability to elicit purity and ward off evil. As food preservation depended greatly on salt before refrigeration, its life-sustaining qualities associated it with auspiciousness in many cultures. Stories, folklore, and superstitious beliefs thus intertwined salt with magic, luck, protection, and healing.

In the Scottish Highlands, expectant mothers carried salt to ward off evil spirits. Newborn babies were gently rubbed with salt to protect them before baptism. Scottish grooms traditionally put a sack of salt on their backs while entering the marital home to bless the couple with luck and financial stability. After that, a handful of salt thrown over the shoulder for good fortune became customary at weddings across Britain. Strong associations of salt with prosperity and blessing can be evidenced across British Isle folklore.

Similarly, bread and salt are essential to traditional Hungarian greetings–with visitors being offered the gifts to symbolize hospitality and divine providence. A fable also says that demons lurk beneath walnut trees and can only be warded off if circled with a rope of human hair and salt. The mineral indeed features in Hungarian stories, greeting customs, and rural superstitions as a guardian against misfortune.

In the Portuguese countryside, widespread beliefs encompass salt's defensive and healing properties against dark magic and ailments. Townspeople craft ritual Floor X-crosses from blessed palm leaves and salt to protect children by placing them under beds. To cure common problems like ear infections, warmed salt wrapped in cloth is gently pressed against afflicted areas while making the cross sign. These rural salted healing rituals continue to be practiced secretly despite official Catholic discouragement.

Among Italians, too, vestiges of ancient spiritual traditions endure through superstitious salt use–with varying regional adaptations. To escape lousy luck, Neapolitans keep salt cellars on dining tables religiously. At the same time, Romans toss handfuls over their left shoulder—Sicilians slide salt sachets into wallet pockets to prevent losses and poverty. From warding off the evil eye to keeping hungry ghosts at bay, Italian salt-based superstitions draw from millennia of myth and lore.

Mummification processes pioneered by the Ancient Egyptians relied heavily on natron–a naturally occurring sodium carbonate salt to rapidly dry corpses for preservation. The mineral's association with resisting decay and passage into the afterlife perpetuated mystical beliefs about its purifying essence across Africa over generations.

Many adherents of Candomblé, an Afro-Brazilian syncretic religion based on Yoruba, Fon, and Bantu faiths brought by African slaves, use salt to claim protection from vengeful spirits of the dead. Ritual foot baths with Epsom salts enable spiritual cleansing before entering sacred spaces. Practitioners additionally employ salt circles to guard against black magic and curses. Hence, salt protects African diaspora devotees during trance, divination, and animal sacrifices.

In the colonial Americas, Native tribes sprinkled maize kernels with salt, asking the Great Spirit for abundant crops. Hopi rainmaking ceremonies involved a celebrant chewing grains with salt and spraying the mixture into the air with chants invoking rainfall. Salt's fertilizing and sky-calling abilities feature in various indigenous religious rain dances, planting rituals, and harvest festivals across North and South America.

With crystals resembling ice and an innate association with life and afterlife preservation, salt has attracted rich mythological status across faiths. Over time, versatile applications from protective charms to healing agents perpetuated strong ties between salt and spirituality, marked by many ethnographic parallels across humanity's shared instinct to sanctify.

Whether scattered ritually in Greek temples or Aztec sacrificial fires, steeped in Sufi wisdom, or the Bible as a purifying metaphor. This unique mineral's intrinsic whiteness, hardness, and permanence have sparked creation stories, magical beliefs, auspicious connotations, and sacred wonder throughout civilizations across time and place.

Chapter 10

The Chemical Revolution: New Processes and Forms

A Pinch of Chemistry: Early Innovations

For thousands of years, salt production remained a straightforward process of solar evaporation or boiling brine. This changed in the 1700s as scientific curiosity about the world extended to the microscopic properties of common minerals like sodium chloride. Early chemists began cataloging different "species" of salts, noticing variances in taste, solubility, and reactions.

In 1736, a French chemistry teacher named Joseph Henri Demeste analyzed a sample from a saltwork and made a revolutionary discovery–ordinary salt contained a second substance, marine acid salt. This compound explained the bitter taste of certain sea salts compared to purer varieties. Demeste's finding sparked interest in further analyzing salt at a molecular level instead of viewing it as a homogeneous substance.

Other seminal insights soon followed. The discovery of new chemicals like hydrochloric acid and sodium carbonate from salt crystals opened up new possibilities for industrial applications. Visionaries dreamed of manufacturing bleach, glass, soap, and dozens of other products dependent on these basic salt derivatives on a grand scale. However, the existing means of procuring salt through labor-intensive pans, mines, or seasonal harvesting were far too small and inconsistent to supply these burgeoning chemical endeavors. New methods would need to be created to extract higher volumes of purer salt.

The first innovations centered around rapidly concentrating brine rather than relying on the sun's heat. In 1775, an ambitious young British technologist named John Thorncroft designed an enclosed system of pans and pipes that used coal fire to distill brine into crystallized salt quickly. Despite numerous technical flaws, Thorncroft's promising prototype inspired others to iterate and improve salt-boiling contraptions throughout the turn of the century.

Soon, the chemical roots of salt would irreversibly reshape how it was sourced and applied on industrial and commercial scales. But the journey was just beginning, with these initial discoveries scratching the surface of sodium chloride's many unique properties and derivatives, waiting to be uncovered through further scientific inquiry and ingenuity. The stage was set for an era where chemistry and salt were more profoundly intertwined than ever before.

Modern Innovations Transform Industry and Society

The seeds of innovation planted in the 1700s bloomed into a new era for salt in the 1800s, catalyzed by visionaries who recognized its potential as both a chemical feedstock and a commodity. An ambitious businessman named Archibald Cochrane stunned England when he used sea salt to manufacture bleaching powder unprecedentedly. He exploited a chemical reaction between salt, sulfuric acid, and lime to create calcium hypochlorite, a compound hailed as a miraculously efficient bleaching agent. Cochrane's factory churned out bleaching powder by the ton, demonstrating how the industry could harness basic salt chemistry. Bleached white textiles became an affordable norm, changing fashion overnight.

Meanwhile, the Solvay brothers etched their name into history using salt crystals as the starting point for mass-producing soda ash. Ernest and Alfred Solvay built briskly expanding plants that captured carbon dioxide gas to react with concentrated brine, yielding pure sodium carbonate more economically than traditional methods. With affordable soda ash available bountifully, imaginative minds concocted new recipes using it as an essential ingredient for glass, detergents, paper, pharmaceuticals, and other up-and-coming essentials of civilized modern life.

But society's ballooning appetite for these products created a dilemma—where could mountainous salt piles be sourced for these ravenous new chemical processes? Once seen as practically infinite, the planet's salt reserves strained to meet demand as factories multiplied rapidly across Europe and America.

Fortunately, the 19th century's pie-in-the-sky optimism and knack for audacious engineering provided solutions. Deep shaft mines punch thousands of feet into buried dried seabeds, accessing remnants from prehistoric oceans. Gargantuan quarrying machines tore into massive sedimentary deposits around the world, most notably the ten thousand-year-old remnants beneath Detroit, Michigan. New rail routes spread across the former wilderness, connecting chemical plants to Earth's salt stockpiles. Economies of scale emerged as machinery exponentially accelerated what laborious hands once strained to harvest.

Yet perhaps the most dramatic leap came from an unlikely place—the rural backwaters of New York State. Brothers Charles and John Arthur Busch, proprietors of a struggling salt works, scrambled to reinvent their operation as the Civil War throttled their traditional business. Inspiration struck Charles upon observing the area's oil boom–principles of drilling, pumping, and distillation– could these not also apply to salt brines?

He successfully obtained funding for an innovative device designed to penetrate the earth with thousand-foot shafts, targeting elusive pockets of saturated brine believed to exist deep below the surface. Skeptics scoffed, and locals waited for the spectacle of failure. But success flowed from the ground up when the wells sputtered to life, spewing pressurized brine. The trickle rapidly intensified into columns of liquid wealth, ten times saltier than seawater. Secure from seasons or tides, the wells punched through to vast troves far outstripping traditional pans.

Quickly, this subterranean prospecting craze multiplied, detonating across gasp-inducing maps. Ohio, Kansas, Texas, and California–geologic lotteries where fortunes festered in liquid form, awaiting human craft to unlock their financial possibilities. With drills piercing the continent's unseen nether regions more rapidly than anyone could track or record, the subsequent decades witnessed epic harvesting crusades to funnel sodium chloride in never-ceasing currents into belching chemical plants and evaporating houses.

Of course, the breakneck pace came at devastating costs; few stopped to tally amidst the gold rush. Entire lakes sucked into puddles; forests leveled into dumping pits, aquifers contaminated beyond recovery, gaping sinkholes swallowing the occasional run of bad luck. But such were the overlooked footnotes amidst soaring corporate profits, supercharged industrial muscles rapidly unlocking chemical intricacies, and paying work for eager masses arriving by immigrant ships or dust bowl trucks.

So the modern salt era churned on, shaping every facet of existence from elemental molecules to emerging empires, even if the dashing physical substance long romanticized by history felt diminished into one input amidst many feeding the insatiable beasts at civilization's pinnacle. Its starring role as a political powerhouse may have waned, but salt still silently sat squarely at the center of technologies, economies, and imagined futures, catapulting humanity into uncharted frontiers. Where it goes next remains hand in hand with societal ambitions. Perhaps into inspiring sustainable balances, equitable abundance for all, and unlocking human potential beyond the wildest dreams.

Chapter 11
Industrialization Transforms the Salt Industry

Salt production methods remained largely unchanged for thousands of years. Early techniques relied on the solar evaporation of salty water in coastal areas with ample sunlight. Seawater, or salty lake water, was channeled into a series of shallow ponds through an intricate system of canals and dykes. As shallow water spread over vast flat surfaces under the sun's heat, pure crystallized salt slowly formed over months-long cycles. This solar technique allowed production on a larger scale than boiling briny spring water in pots, enabling the growth of entire industries and economies surrounding salt.

The earliest recorded saltworks likely developed in ancient Mesopotamia. Basins for salt making from the third millennium BCE have been unearthed near ancient sites like Lagash and Ur in modern Iraq. Salt was precious for food preservation, and its production became the domain of temple authorities, who carefully maintained their solar evaporation fields. In ancient economies, salt rations were included in pay for laborers and administrators alike, highlighting its value alongside grain and woven wool. Over two thousand years later, solar evaporation remained the most lucrative salt production method in the arid climate of Mesopotamia.

Similarly, in Ancient Egypt, basins for solar evaporated salt from the Nile Delta appear in early archaeological records before the Old Kingdom around 2500 BCE. Papyri documented large state-controlled saltworks on the northern coasts of the Nile River, with duties overseen by a hierarchy of officials. Salt was used liberally in Egyptian cooking and food preservation, alongside Natron salt mined from dry lake beds for mummification. Its value necessitated a state monopoly and strict record-keeping for production levels. Saltworks built under the earliest pharaohs continued supplying the ingredients critical to ancient Egyptian diets and rituals for over two thousand years.

The ancient Chinese also recognized the importance of domestically produced salt for food security, developing solar evaporation fields as early as 6000 BCE. Along the Yellow River and Yangtze River basins, inland lakes and marshlands provided natural salt sources diverted into man-made evaporation ponds on a growing scale. By 2000 BCE, in the Shang Dynasty, government salt monopolies were firmly established, with production quotas and price controls strictly dictated by the authorities. As one of China's essential commodities alongside rice, tea, silk, and spices, salt merited a designated Salt Commission in the Han Dynasty to govern its production and distribution across the vast empire.

In warmer, drier climes like North Africa and the Mediterranean coast, a slightly different solar technique called salocoction was employed over two thousand years ago. Seawater was channeled into man-made salt pans along sandy shorelines. When enough water evaporated over time, fires were set underneath clay-lined pans to boil off the remaining moisture rapidly. This sped up evaporation, yielding purer dry salt crystals in batches. African salt springs near desert oases also provided briny water similarly boiled into salt using fires and earthen pots. Salocoction required more labor and fuel but less space than coastal evaporation fields. It remained common around the Sahara and North Africa for millennia, as well as in Spain and Southern Europe.

The ancient Indian subcontinent developed multiple methods for salt production, fitting its diverse landscapes. Coastal areas like Gujarat relied on solar evaporation in shallow salt pans identical to those scattered around the Indian Ocean. But inland areas often harvest salty earth, baking the surrounding soil in dried cow dung fuel to filter out pure crystals. Salt extraction from soil, ash, and mineral deposits over wood fires produced characteristically brown, unrefined Indian salts. By the Gupta Empire around 400 CE, the northern and eastern Indian kingdoms had extensive state monopolies over inland mineral salt and coastal sea salt production. Salt taxes added to imperial coffers for centuries, while salt makers inherited their vocation generationally in closed communities.

Similarly, diverse techniques emerged across pre-Columbian Mesoamerica and South America to supply vital salt. The oldest saltworks in North America ran from 700 BCE on Isla Cerritos off the Yucatan Peninsula coast. Maya salt makers diverted seawater into shallow lakes to solar evaporate over time, eventually stacking filled pots to drain off salt crystal slurry. Inland, native peoples sought out natural salt deposits and hot saline springs. Local tribes on the Peru-Bolivia border harvested salt crystallized by the freezing night temperatures of the Andean highlands as early as 1000 BCE at sites like Salinas de Garci Mendoza. Water from natural springs was diverted into hundreds of mountainside pans, and then gleaned for salt daily. Further south, near the Atacama Desert, Inca and Tiwanaku peoples collected prized solar-evaporated salt from the edges of vast saline lakes. Salt also had deep ritual meaning and uses, like the bovine blood sacrifice precinct at Mount Huyana Picchu, highlighting its lasting spiritual impact.

In Europe, three main methods emerged, informed by suitable environments. The Northern and Eastern regions had access to large underground salt deposits directly mined. The earliest salt mines opened around 5400 BCE in Poland, near Krakow, at Wieliczka and Bochnia. For millennia, miners dug tunnels by hand, excavating thick veins of rock salt for ground refining. Central European miners eventually used explosives and water to dissolve solid deposits and horses and oxen to haul salt to the surface. Iconic mines like Hallstatt in the Austrian alps inspired the entire surrounding economic regions, which were reliant on the essential mineral. Coastal areas like Northern France instead crafted shallow salt evaporation ponds filled by the sea, harvesting salt when waters retreated low enough to expose the glittering beds awaiting collection. Celtic tribes traded the gray sea salt through regional exchange routes across the British Isles and Northern Europe as early as 500 BCE. Meanwhile, around the Mediterranean, solar and salococcion techniques reigned supreme. The Romans integrated salt production deeply into their sprawling civilization. Provinces from Hispania to North Africa and Bythinia to Lusitania specialized in mass salt production both inland and on the coasts to supply the Romans' notorious love of salt fish sauces and conserve preservation.

By the early Middle Ages, salt production infrastructure across Asia, Africa, and Europe was well established to meet local demands. Techniques had changed little in over four thousand years. Regional production centers around salt lakes, marshes, springs, and mines were carefully maintained. Salt remained essential for growing nations and empires alongside grain, metal, livestock, and spices. Its unique value stems from the labor and time-intensive processes required to harvest it and its enduring utility for preserving meat and fish stocks. As food became globalized through the increased reach of stable empires and trade routes, salt paved the way as a commodity and a means to trade further abroad. With European powers ramping up naval and merchant exploration from the 15th century, salt's usefulness became twofold. They required regular salt supplies for their ships' stores to ensure preservation on long voyages while trading salt and related techniques with cultures worldwide.

This marked the gradual transition towards industrialization as globalization exposed more lucrative markets abroad, and rising populations demanded more salt for food. Various innovations emerged in response—China developed deep borehole drilling to extract underground brine around 1100 CE during the Song Dynasty rule, which was refined into exploding popularity through natural gas wells in the late 1800s. Coastal salt ponds added windmills and lever systems to help regulate sluice gate flows. New trades like the saunders of France meticulously refined sea salt in diverse grades for various uses in kitchens and dining halls. Yet core solar evaporation, boiling, and mining continued to dominate where local environments allowed. These three pillars of natural salt harvesting persisted even in early factories. The first mechanized salt works in Europe relying on steam engines emerged in the mid-1700s in England and Germany. However, they still focused on refining mined salt or finalizing the solar evaporation process through artificial heat.

Over the long arc of human civilization, salt production remained closely tied to local water sources and fuel supplies through early modern times, before the advent of electric light and power. Strategies tailored to regional terrain offered relative continuity in techniques over millennia, compared to disruptions in contemporary food, medicine, tools, and more. The very consistency of laborious solar evaporation, salt mining, and boiling linked humanity across ages. Though chains grew longer between producer and consumer as cities swelled and empires expanded, the basic harvest of this essential mineral persisted. Its global journeys reflected not sudden innovation but gradual trade infrastructure, enabling salt's worldwide reach after originating from those enduring sources—the sun-drenched sea, the dark mines welled deep in the mountains, the small flame-kindling white crystals out of springs.

The seeds of disruption took root in the salt industry as Enlightenment ideals shaped mechanical innovations across Europe. Scientists sought to understand salt's unique chemical properties and derive new production methods. Engineers drafted plans for steam-powered pumps and evaporators. Investors assembled capital to build hulking factories. Yet traditional salt makers clung to time-honored techniques even as industrialization loomed.

In England, visionary salt industrialist John Thomson spearheaded the push towards mechanized production starting in the 1790s. Mineral salt from ancient mines in Cheshire had long supplied the realm, but demand constantly strained supply. Thomson erected the first steam-powered saltworks near Liverpool, using coal to boil brine rapidly. His polished salt bricks proved popular for provisioning British naval ships and merchant vessels. Yet just as Thomson's salt works succeeded, Napoleon Bonaparte's blockade of England in the early 1800s cut off vital imports of Spanish salt for the Southern market. Scrambling merchants like Samuel Waring dusted off abandoned plans for steam pump systems to force water through disused Staffordshire salt mines. New rows of pans bolstered by coal and steam refined saturated brines without solar evaporation. England's salt supply gained hard-fought resilience against instability abroad.

In France, too, ambitious saltwork owners like Nicolas Leblanc petitioned the post-Revolution state to support new chemical means for domestic salt production. Solar coastal works stood vulnerable to foreign conflict and blockade. Leblanc proposed using sulfuric acid to break down salt-rich soils into soda ash solutions, which were then precipitated into pure salts. His fragmented success spurred further state funding after the Napoleonic Wars peaked. Government programs brought university chemists and private investors together to optimize techniques for extracting salt from inland salt springs through acid treatments.

The proliferation of coal mines and steam engines across Central Europe also drove visionary salt barons like Germany's Carl Julius Graf von Ballestrem. Since the Middle Ages, Polish royalty has guarded rich salt deposits in Galacia, stifling development elsewhere. Ballestrem boldly erected new factories in 1828, harnessing steam and coal to distill salt via boiling and chemical processes from deep boreholes through Saxony's rocky crust. His first brine well at Rheine pumped potent mineral waters to the surface through cast iron pipes and innovative pumping systems to supply neighboring chemical works. This kicked off Germany's industrial salt revolution, as traditional solar works struggled to compete with the volumes of pure, cheap salt churned out by wagon loads from around the Ruhr region.

Even in the New World, changes percolated across North America's wild salt frontiers. Underground salt deposits attracted entrepreneurs to backbreaking efforts to manually pump up the brine, fuel shallow boilers with wood, and burn massive amounts of timber. The War of 1812 highlighted the embryonic country's reliance on imported salt when supplies were interrupted. Responding to the threat, President Andrew Jackson signed federal land grants in 1841 to ignite investment in domestic salt production. Edward Pennington capitalized on steam power by installing coal-hungry engines across Pennsylvania and Virginia salt furnaces in the 1840s to drive pipeline pumps.

Yet traditional solar production persisted despite an encroaching industry, retaining distinction in sunnier climes. By the late 1800s, the Andalusian coast was scattered with over two hundred modest saltworks crafting Spain's famed flor de sal using well-worn medieval techniques. Further south, Cape Verde's remote solar salt islands have powered the economy since Portuguese colonial days. Industrial competitors found traction harder in warmer continents as reliable sea and sun continued feeding families. Cottage salt works coexisted alongside disruptive factories reshaping familiar city skylines in England and Germany, though the two worlds remained ignorant of each other's boons or ills.

Mechanized salt works brought prosperity at the cost of laborers' welfare and environmental damage. Sites like Droyßig, Germany, soaked up coal and construction capital while exposing workers to acids and steam leaks. Propitiating mine explosions and machinery accidents haunted production quotas. Yet, market pressures also deteriorated traditional livelihoods, like in Sumatra's Aceh province. Declining harvests pushed Tamil salt farmers towards unsafe deep-sea diving for salt crusts, risking decompression sickness and shark attacks despite Hindu beliefs forbidding seawater contact. Customs died hard for those raised harvesting salt beneath open skies rather than around sooty, hissing contraptions.

Industrialization's rosy promises held equal parts peril for traditional salt symbols now waning against modern factories. The pace of disruptive change shuffled social orders and salt-making families. Yet salt's essential nature could not be ignored; wherever industry fell short, solar and artisanal works provisioned local communities using weathered techniques. New methods churned out salt in unprecedented volumes, but venerated wisdom lingered in the hands of those weathering storms and scraping salt pans generationally. The uneasy juxtaposition between timeless production and fickle mechanical innovation would only widen through the technological leaps of the coming decades.

Chapter 12

Mahatma Gandhi's Salt March Against Colonial Rule

Among the twentieth-century freedom struggles to topple the age of empires, few campaigns proved more pivotal or internationally galvanizing than one elderly ascetic's 24-day, 240-mile walk challenging monopoly control over nature's most essential mineral gift along India's western shores in 1930. Brandishing a fistful of illegal sea salt before thunderous crowds from Dandi to Dharasana, Mohandas Gandhi sparked a wave of mass civil disobedience, eventually forcing the world's mightiest empire to its knees and birthing independent India through ultimately non-violent defiance. If ever a condiment played an unlikely starring role in changing global history, the Salt Satyagraha stands foremost.

Gandhi's masterstroke of using salt to stir rebellion derived from practical and symbolic genius. Practically, the 1882 British Salt Tax, which applied steep tariffs even on natural sea salt, devastated average Indians through what amounted to an essential dietary tax. This hit the poorest majority already living at the subsistence level hardest, forcing difficult tradeoffs over buying basic salt to supplement bland staples against other necessities like clothing or lamp oil. Such daily kitchen worries offered relatable outrage, fanning mass sympathy for the anti-tax campaign in villages countrywide.

Symbolically, Gandhi instilled deeper resonance by framing salt rights as the moral basis for wider self-rule. The British claim that underground salt from India's sacred seas rightfully belonged to the Colonial Office rather than her people, who carried an arrogant aura of declaring sovereignty over the land. Unjust salt policy thereby encapsulated imperial exploitation generally, touching Indians personally in the most routine privations while confiscatory taxes transported wealth overseas without the consent of the governed. Hence, reclaiming salt through Gandhian civil disobedience–making and selling it illegally–enacted on a small scale, the wholesale independence struggle boiling nationwide following broken British promises of home rule after the Great War.

The Salt March originated soon after the 1929 New Year Declaration of Independence when Gandhi proposed escalating the Indian Home Rule movement by directly targeting unfair commodity taxes, which formed a pillar of British rule. On March 12, 1930, Gandhi set off from his religious retreat at Sabarmati, near Ahmedabad, towards the coast, some 240 miles distant, with 78 devout ashramites. Reaching villages along the route, he addressed swelling crowds, urging peaceful defiance once his small band began ceremonially making salt at the journey's end to render the tax obsolete through open mass violation. Even while trekking strictly adhering to ascetic discipline–rising before dawn for prayer, wearing the simplest handspun shawls, walking shoeless, and cooking his meals over an open fire–Gandhi enthralled growing audiences with a quiet dignity that soon radiated globally.

By April 5th, when Gandhi's band arrived at the seaside village of Dandi, thousands awaited what headlines were already branding his 'Salt Rebellion'. Wading knee-deep into the brine, the 61-year-old mahatma ritualistically scooped up a palmful of muddy salt while reciting a prayer, technically completing the criminal transgression. He implored spectators similarly to commence civilly breaking the law by illegally evaporating or selling sea salt. Nonviolent satyagraha protests erupted almost instantly up and down India's long coastlines. Millions enthusiastically boiled seawater, evading steep taxation that had monopolized life's most basic seasoning for generations. Such sweeping participation signaled salt's power to mobilize mass non-cooperation.

Predictably, authorities pushed back forcefully, determined to crush defiance towards British economic controls. Over 60,000 Indians were jailed that year, including nearly the entire senior Home Rule leadership, while police ransacked villages, confiscating contraband and unleashing beatings that killed hundreds nationwide. The worst brutality occurred at Dharasana Salt Works in May, when colonial police mercilessly clubbed unresisting Indian volunteers, mostly to death, before horrified foreign journalists under orders to clamp down on illegal production. But rather than quelling unrest, outrage, and bad publicity alarmed officials in London, fearing international opinion and America's support for independence might turn decisively against their absent concessions.

When the embattled Viceroy Lord Irwin finally invited Gandhi to negotiate a truce in early 1931 after a year of instability, salt provided the centerpiece symbolism again for peace talks. Recognizing both sides' humanity, the two leaders together produced illegal salt from the seas at Gandhi's ashram as an act of reconciliation before broader governance reforms. This *Pact with the Devil'* bitterly divided loyalists yet re-energized nationwide civil disobedience that forced major British rollbacks by the decade's end. A decade later, as colonial rule crumbled amid postwar bankruptcy, Gandhi's strategic use of salt in cornering world opinion through nonviolent tactics pointed to India's path to securing independence in 1947 without the need for large-scale violence. His salt satyagraha introduced the world to civil rights resistance that inspired movements from US segregation protests to Eastern European democratic revolutions decades later.

Today, with its salt marshes and pilgrimage route, Dandi holds almost mythic significance in India's foundational lore, comparable to where the American Revolution began at Lexington and Concord. The humble spot marking Gandhi's transcendent lawbreaking draws Indian leaders annually, commemorating that decisive stroke against imperialism enabled by Nature's humble mineral. And fittingly, in 2002, on the Salt March's 70th anniversary, India's president abolished the remaining vestiges of the notorious tax itself as independent India came full circle, honoring Mahatma Gandhi's exemplary use of salt crystallizing dissent into eventual liberation.

Chapter 13

Salt in 20th-Century Politics and Conflict

The First Stirrings of Revolt

As the 20th century dawned, salt remained a coveted commodity subject to taxes and restrictions across numerous empires, just as it had for millennia. However, new ideas about governance, autonomy, and human rights were beginning to take hold worldwide. In some cases, the salt policy became a flashpoint for growing resentment against imperial rule.

In India's interior, far from the coasts, the arid climate made salt difficult to come by. Yet the British Raj maintained a strict salt monopoly and enforced it violently when challenged. When Gandhi started his civil disobedience campaign in 1930, his symbolic Salt March to the seaside electrified the nation. But discontent had already been simmering over salt taxes for years prior. In 1908, the local ethnic Pashtun tribe revolted against fines for unauthorized salt production. The British forces crushed the uprising viciously, wiping out villages in a campaign the tribesmen still recount with bitterness today.

Similarly, in Central Asia, Tsarist salt policies spurred public outrage in the years before Russia's 1917 revolution. Salt mining and distribution had long been a state monopoly, with private salt trading legally categorized as smuggling. While salt-smuggling sentences were usually limited to warnings or small fines, public whippings were common. These sparked public outcry, especially when religious minorities were targeted.

1912 Russian administrators announced a major salt tax hike to fund new military battleships. This inflamed public sentiment among Central Asia's poorest Muslims, who already viewed Russian salt policies as an injustice. Numerous protests broke out, with Russian Cossacks dispersing demonstrators by force. The tax was eventually imposed regardless, leaving a residual bitterness that historians argue laid fertile ground for the Bolshevik revolutionary message.

Taxation Triggers Turmoil

Salt taxation has provoked fierce resistance across Latin America over the past century. In 1902, protests against a new salt tax in Colombia escalated into the Thousand Days War, one of the region's most destructive civil conflicts. The salt tax hit subsistence farmers hard while exempting wealthier households.

Riots soon morphed into a full-scale peasant uprising against oligarchic rule. Marauding bands burned tax registers and raided government salt warehouses. Violent salt riots continued in some areas even after the war ended in 1903. The Chilean government was forced to station troops along its borders to halt smuggled salt.

Similarly, El Salvador's indigenous people, the Pipil, revolted against repeated hikes in the nation's salt tax starting in 1915. Salt was scarce in the mountainous inland regions where most Pipil lived, meaning the tax burden fell heaviest on the poor. After a fresh salt tax was announced in 1931, the Pipil took up arms. Their 1932 indigenous rebellion left up to 30,000 dead before government troops achieved victory through scorched earth tactics.

Throughout the 1930s, new or increased salt taxes ignited popular fury across Latin America. Mexico's indigenous Zapotec people rose in 1937 when salt monopolies were expanded, as did Guatemalan peasants in 1934 when a salt tax was decreed to fund new schools. In Peru, a state salt monopoly imposed in 1938 led to riots in Cusco. Opponents argued it would disproportionately harm Quechua mountain dwellers struggling to purchase the essential mineral.

Salt Smuggling as Social Protest

Like taxes on tea, tobacco, and sugar, salt taxes have always engendered smuggling. However, illicit salt trading has often carried greater moral weight thanks to salt's life-sustaining qualities. Gandhi's 1930 salt march, which began by symbolically evaporating seawater to produce salt illegally, sparked nationwide sympathy by framing salt taxes as an injustice against India's poorest citizens.

In the Caribbean, salt smuggling, aided by transnational networks, became an act of defiance against colonial rule. By the mid-20th century, the United Kingdom maintained lucrative salt monopolies and associated taxes across islands like Jamaica, Grand Turk, and the Bahamas, vestiges of 18th-century British sea power. Islanders frequently relied on smuggled U.S. salt, distributed via small boats under the cover of night.

Locals saw illicit American salt as more than pocketbook savings; it enabled them to provide for their families while flouting imperial taxes. In Jamaica, salt smuggling surged in the late 1950s as the independence movement grew. It became intertwined with the broader struggle against British exploitation of the islands.

Similarly, in West Africa, salt smuggling fueled anti-colonial resistance. France maintained a total monopoly over Senegal's salt supply, and salt prices were extremely inflated compared to surrounding territories. By 1947, illegal Ghanaian and Portuguese salt comprised 80% of the salt consumed locally. French authorities launched violent crackdowns, but Senegalese citizens and leaders defended smuggling as morally justified resistance.

Senegal's first president and famed poet, Léopold Senghor, captured the public sentiment in his 1948 poem Salt, evoking salt smugglers as dignified freedom fighters whose actions encapsulated popular defiance of unjust monopolies more broadly: "They advance like fate...with the step of conscience assured and faces resolute."

The Global March Towards Reform

By the mid-20th century, attitudes around governance shifted as European empires crumbled. Newly independent nations in Asia and Africa often avoided salt taxes and monopolies or enacted reforms. Yet, in pockets of Latin America, salt policy continued to provoke turbulence even through the late 1900s.

Most famously, in Bolivia, public outcry over sharp hikes in salt taxes detonated massive national strikes in 1959 and again in 1987. The 1987 protests succeeded in ousting the military regime after six weeks of paralyzing civil resistance led by trade unions. In Mexico, indigenous movements targeted salt price increases into the 1990s, arguing that high salt costs disproportionately impacted impoverished mountain communities.

However, from the late 20th century onward, large-scale salt policy clashes have dwindled globally. Market liberalization, decentralization of tax powers, and greater representation for marginalized groups have defused much of the tensions historically tied to state salt policies. Salt smuggling, too, loses its subversive edge when tariffs disappear and borders open to free trade.

Yet echoes of salt unrest still occasionally surface, revealing the mineral's lasting power to inflame passions tied to social justice, even while its necessity fades for wealthy nations. In 2014 and 2018, fresh salt riots broke out unexpectedly in India and Haiti over new levies on the essential spice once pivotal for national budgets. More than any staple, something innately provocative lingers around salt and taxation that transcends the mere economics at play. Because behind the salt policy, the bitter taste of injustice and impaired sovereignty is never too distant, no matter how much progress unfolds. This vulnerability was ruthlessly exploited in later centuries during the frequent wars ravaging Renaissance Italy. Enemy states like Genoa and Milan would blockade or sabotage Venice's vital Adriatic salt fleets arriving from Istria and Dalmatia. Doge chroniclers described the "wasting misery" and "general despair" in the streets each time salt stockpiles ran dry. Shipments of grain and cured meats are putrefied without salt for preservation. Hungry citizens even looted the salt stores of Venetian nobles during the War of Chioggia famine in 1380.

The most devastating siege in history remains Leningrad's near-death over 900 days between 1941 and 1944. The Axis chokehold severed all routes for food, fuel, and industrial salt vital to the city's munitions plants. Each month, over 100,000 civilians perished, as many from starvation as Nazi shelling. Workers at the Koyrovsky salt plant labored and emaciated under siege bombardment to provide sodium chlorate for Leningrad's arms factories. "We were famished, but we knew salt was vital, so we worked on..." wrote engineer Ignat Danilov before tragically starving to death himself in 1942. It was salt workers who survived at the lowest rates in this horrifying siege. But Leningrad clung on, thanks partly to their labors, until relief arrived– at the cost of 1.5 million lives.

Salt's recurring significance during human conflicts underscores its invisible influence over civilization. As with past eras, salt remains woven into the present world order's fabric in myriad ways modern societies scarcely contemplate. But this benign mineral retains its formidable power to shape humanity's fate in disruptive ways if supplies fall into jeopardy again. The ripple effects risk unleashing chaos once more.

India on the Brink of Starvation

In newly independent India, the young nation balanced dangerously with famine after partition riots and refugee flows disrupted harvests and infrastructure in 1947-48. The crisis even threatened nuclear conflagration as India and Pakistan almost entered war over disputed Kashmir. But beneath the headlines, chronic salt scarcity nearly proved more immediately catastrophic for India.

Pakistan's exit slashed India from major saltworks, which Islamabad now controls in the Indus River plains. These supplied over 80% of the subcontinent's salt previously, heavily impacting the winter pickling of vegetables and fruit that conserved essential vitamins. Salinity also fell drastically due to dwindling cattle stocks in northern villages. Officials estimated salt availability would plunge to 90% for certain Indian provinces in the coming months without emergency action. Gandhi foresaw disaster, warning the new Congress Prime Minister by telegram: "Next to air and water, salt is perhaps the greatest necessity of life."

Some observers believed Pakistan intended salt access denial as a deliberate policy to weaken India through mass civilian deaths. While likely untrue, India initially feared this "as a great or even greater danger than war" (Nehru). But crash efforts to import salt averted catastrophe by late 1948, though stemming further losses from continued inter-communal violence proved harder as millions uprooted by terror attacks lost livelihoods.

The survival struggles of Partition reflected salt's silent sway over stability once supply ebbs. India stood historically no stranger to the intimate link between salt scarcity and societal breakdown, as Gandhi understood deeply from the broken British salt promises that fueled his independence movement decades earlier.

Salt Scarcity Spurs Regional Rivalries

The interwoven relationship between salt supply and geopolitics grew more complex after decolonization in the mid-century, birthed numerous landlocked nations across Central Asia and Africa. With no direct salt sources, these countries relied on porous borders and open markets. This fostered new rivalries, with coastal neighbors holding power over inland populations through potential salt embargoes.

Such tensions simmer today around Uganda, which imports 95% of its salt demand from Kenya's ports at Mombasa and Malaba. This lifeline stretches back to colonial times, underscoring how arbitrary European map-making endures stirring trouble. Worries about over-dependence flare up sporadically amid poor relations between the East African nations. Smuggling is rife while prices fluctuate wildly in Ugandan markets with each about of regional tensions. But rationing risks catalyzing chaos, as seen in 1966 when Idi Amin's soldiers revolted violently over salt rations halved by half.

The recent discovery of modest salt springs in Uganda's Katwe crater offers meager insurance as population pressures continue climbing.

The Caspian Sea forms another hotspot where clashes over salt seem ever waiting to erupt. Iran controls a majority of its waters after the Soviet Union's demise fractured the coastline between new countries. Yet blockading salt remains taboo, given that minority Azeri and Turkmen regions have depended heavily on Caspian salt fish for income and sustenance since ancient times. Salt in local cuisine carries tremendous cultural weight.

But Tehran risks future naval quarantines if Azerbaijan's nationalist and Islamist opposition ever gain power, while Turkmenistan's autocracy eyes making risky regional power plays as gas wealth mounts. For now, informal salt supply accords endure between three capitals united by Shi'a Muslim affinity. But the world may yet rue the day Caspian salt commerce flows in anger once again. Because societies survive cross-border bondage better than broken salt promises.

Sodium Chloride Curses and Human Folly

Beyond bodily needs, salt's mineral essence carries a deeper meaning for people worldwide, as spiritual traditions attest. Salt covenants held inviolable power around sharing meals in history, anchoring bonds sworn before deities. Even in modern times, oath breakers risked fearful salt curses promising bad fortune or death in some cultures. Perhaps it is no surprise that perfidies around war and salt through time ignite higher passions towards justice.

So, while chemical explanations now clarify salt's role in muscle and neuron functioning, its otherworldly qualities still ignite human imagination outside pure physiology. Portuguese sailors traditionally evoked the legend of 'dom Sebastião'-- a quixotic monarch forever attempting to return home– if they spilled salt at sea. Ominously though, superstition promised eternal maritime damnation for those who broke vows after 'sealing the deal' over spilt salt.

Among Himalayan tribes like the Gurung of Nepal, passing salt to guests means automatic protection from enemies under the snow peaks their faiths inhabit. Giving salt water to departing visitors ensures prosperity upon their return through obligations conferred by the ancient spirits. Perhaps this explains Nepalis' fierce resistance to blocking salt supplies on high passes when China imposed its 1960s blockade over border disputes and halted caravans. Though vastly outweighed militarily, Nepal held certain mountain terrain long enough for secret nighttime salt convoys until Beijing relented.

In the debugger world's high-stakes standoffs, the language of sodium chloride still occasionally reveals undertones of magical thinking seemingly incongruous amid sophisticated realpolitik. Yet when diplomacy and deterrence falter, hope always remains for miraculous reversals of fate. Unless leaders rashly destroy salt contracts binding people in unseen ways, no tanks or treaties encompass them. Where bonds linger, providence demands that salt promises hold.

Chapter 14

Salt in the Modern Diet: Too Much of a Good Thing?

Once valued as a precious commodity, salt has taken on a more controversial status in our modern age. Yet it retains an enduring omnipresence on tables and ingredient lists around the world.. While salt maintains its crave-able quality on the tongue, its health impacts compel moderation.

The Rise of Salt as Commonplace Seasoning

Salt's potent preservative power allowed earlier civilizations to sustain themselves through harsh winters and long journeys. However storage limitations and production difficulties kept it precious for centuries. That rarity etched an affinity for salt on the human palate—a biological imprint that still lingers today. The Tongan phrase "toa'aso'o kai pulu moli"—literal translation "eager like cows to salt dust"—affirms salt's enduring allure. Yet sprinkling salt atop dishes grew increasingly commonplace over time, stripping away some of its coveted mystique. This transition emerged most prominently in Europe from the late Middle Ages into the Early Modern period. More organized salt mining and refining growth bolstered supply levels across communities. Rising trade activity also funneled salt inland along roadways from bustling port cities. By the 18th century, the average European consumed up to 50 grams of salt daily—on par with most modern guidelines. Yet this salty shift took far longer across North America due to its decentralized, rural nature. The Erie Canal's opening brought the first large-scale salt shipments into the American interior in 1825. Within 25 years, per capita consumption doubled to over 12 pounds annually. By the early 1900s, European settlers had fully imparted their saline affinity onto the New World.

From Scarcity to Excess– Changing Perceptions as Production Modernizes

Beyond geographical or infrastructural limits, taxes also once placed salt out of reach for the common folk. As a lucrative source of revenue for regimes from China to France, salt stimulated smuggling when prices overwhelmed peasants' purses. However, the growth of industrialization helped slacken the governmental grip on salt supplies. Innovations like steam-powered pumps and artificial evaporation boosted global production tenfold between the early 1800s and World War I. Coinciding social shifts also removed salt taxes one by one, as French revolutionaries gave the first call to end the gabelle in 1790. Yet, as salt became abundantly accessible, perceptions evolved. Its potency for preserving meat had marked salt as a stalwart companion for nomads across Siberia or sailors out to sea. However, the advent of refrigeration and canning towards the end of the 19th century removed salt from this pedestal. As the modern processed food industry expanded, salt slipped stealthily into staples like bread, crackers, and cheese. Today, we consume over 75% of our salt "invisibly" through manufactured goods. This dissolved the conscious connection between seasoning and preservation—a link deeply ingrained over generations. And so salt transitioned from a deliberate dose added sparingly at the table to a behind-the-scenes infiltrator flooding our food system en masse.

Current Salt Consumption– Guidelines and Global Intake Realities

Most public health bodies suggest limiting salt intake to under 6 grams daily, equal to about one teaspoon. Some figures fall closer to the 3-4 gram range as research continues to probe salt's health impacts. Yet global consumption currently triples most maximum recommendations. The average intake hovers around 10 grams daily worldwide, extending up to 15 grams in salt-loving countries like China and Thailand. This gap between suggested and actual salt consumption informs global strategies today. Campaigns across Argentina, Japan, and the UK have targeted packaged, prepared, and served foods to reduce their salt content gradually. Finland is a success story where a boost in public awareness and food industry buy-in has lowered average consumption by over 40%. However, these gradual gains continue to swim against the rising tides of fast food and busy lifestyles dependent on convenience choices high in hidden salt. India offers perhaps the most intriguing case of a booming economy wrestling to balance public health with an ingrained penchant for salt. Despite nationwide efforts to curtail excessive salt use, traditional pickles, chutneys, and spices bolster India's average intake. This signals the ultimate need for culturally-tailored strategies targeting population segments rather than one-size-fits-all global recommendations. Because of all of the salt's potential ills, it remains a legendary substance rooted deeply in humanity's tastes and traditions across civilizations, present and past.

Chapter 15

The Future of Salt Production and Technology

The sun-baked salt pans glimmered as far as the eye could see. Manuel gazed across the geometric patchwork of ponds, envisioning the harvest ahead. For decades, his family had labored to extract salt from these arid coastal flats, using manual tools and timeworn methods passed down through generations. But this year, things will be different.

New, gleaming machinery had arrived—strange pumps, filters, and crystallizers Manuel scarcely understood. Yet the engineers assured him these devices would transform antiquated salt cultivation into a modern, efficient operation. Initially, Manuel felt skeptical about tampering with generations of hard-won experience. But the world was changing quickly. If the livelihood of his community was to survive, they needed to embrace the future.

Manuel felt hopeful yet anxious as he watched the technicians assemble the pipework around the pans. Would these shining metallic contraptions extract salt more productively from the precious brine they had always relied on? Or would tinkering with the time-hallowed ways backfire, upending the community's sole industry? Only time would tell whether this union of machine and mineral would yield a bountiful new age of salt for the village.

The prospect of enhancing production has motivated innovations in salt harvesting technology for millennia. Yet recently, global population growth and rising demand have accelerated the impetus for efficient, high-volume output. With over 215 million tonnes now produced annually, salt is one of the world's most widely exploited minerals. Many regions still utilize traditional, labor-intensive approaches derived from centuries of wisdom. However, escalating market pressures are catalyzing a wave of technological upgrades worldwide.

In Europe's Alpine heartland, families who have sourced medicinal salt from mountain mines for generations are adopting advanced drilling and transport systems. Cavernous new tunnels are bored effortlessly into seams of rock salt by laser-guided boreheads. Remote-controlled shuttle pods whisk the precious crystals to underground grinding stations. Automated processors wash, mill, and package the salt, readying the batches for international export. Workers who once wielded pickaxes by candlelight now marshal LED-lit control rooms. Yet, despite radical innovations, the soulful healing lore surrounding these mythical salt lodes persists.

Along northern Africa's Mediterranean coastline, solar evaporation farms have dramatically modernized salt production. Here, shallow seaside pools once dotted the landscape—lovingly tended by farmers who channeled brine and coaxed salt from the sun's rays. Today, many outmoded saltpans have merged into mega-operations lining the coast. Banks of pumped brine now circulate rapidly around vast squared grids of concentrator ponds. These industrial panoramas are drone-mapped and satellite-tracked to optimize salinity and yield. Robot-guided harvesters traverse the ponds, sieving crystallized salt 24 hours a day.

Yet, for all the gadgets and efficiencies, veteran workers insist that fine sea salt retains an aura from its marshland origins. Under the billowing sheets of plastic shielding many evaporation steps from contaminants, they still recall the joy of guiding salty crystals amid birdsong and ocean breezes. Their mechanical replacements cannot mimic the subtle art of enhancing texture and mineral balance. Thus, despite bold leaps in bulk processing power, traditionalists maintain some heirloom harvesting methods by hand– if merely for the salts' more rarified gourmet niches.

This reluctant truce between technology and tradition now characterizes salt production worldwide. Innovations have undoubtedly unlocked enormous productivity gains in extraction, processing, and distribution. Yet, whether delving veins of rock salt, channeling brine, or harnessing the sun's heat, many communities cling to time-honored techniques that honor salts' rich histories. Though machinery mainlines tons of standardized salt daily onto grocers' shelves, boutique methods persist for the most refined grades. Thus, technology has come to partner but has not yet usurped the generations of cherished salt-making lore.

Sea Salt Bioreactors: Harnessing Ocean Microbes

As global demand for gourmet sea salt climbs, some innovative Pacific companies cultivate boutique salt crystals using bioreactors that house communities of salt-loving marine microorganisms. Within these glassy vats, IM-grade seawater circulates rapidly synthesizing archaea and halophilic bacteria. Programmed nutrient injections stimulate specialized species to draw ionic minerals from the swirling brine into budding nano-scale compartments. Over 72 hours, these salty vesicles develop intricate lattice structures ideal for forming subtle, flavored salts. Finally, automated UV triggers rupture the microbe clusters, releasing thousands of tiny cubic-salt crystals ready for gentle sun drying. Though yields per bioreactor barely match a coastal evaporation pond, epicurean chefs swear these complex living salts gift seafood and meat with unrivaled tastes.

Some biotech startups now advocate scaling up microbe-grown sea salts in buried offshore bioreactors, using renewable tidal power for circulation. Proponents claim networked clusters of these brine-filled pods could sustainably generate sought-after flavors and flower salts year-round. However, opponents argue manipulating marine microbe ecosystems risks long-term harm, especially if single-product strains dominate. Conservationists urge further studies, though gourmand investors seem eager to launch demonstration bioreactor rigs offshore. If successful, these submerged salt factories could upend solar production that relies on capricious weather. But what unexpected changes might arise from industrializing tiny ancient lifeforms that evolved in balance with ocean ecology?

Salt-Based Data Storage: When Crystals Never Forget

As global data generation explodes, quantum computer scientists believe ultra-stable salt crystals could provide virtually eternal data archival systems to supplement overloaded server farms. By laser-etching micro-size grains of pure synthetic salt with polarized fractures encoding bit-data, researchers recently stored vast archives that survived over 5 years completely intact. Such non-volatile 'salty bytes' resist heat, radiation, and moisture far better than magnetic drives or SSDs. If temperature and humidity stay relatively low, salt-stored datasets may persist and be preserved for centuries without degradation.

Several governments now fund proof-of-concept eternal data vaults carved deep into salt mine caverns lined with alkali-metal halide memory crystals. If successful, almost limitless data could endure safely beneath mountains or oceans encoded in sextillions of microscopic, salty file cabinets. Startups race to develop rapid optical writers to inscribe petabytes of records economically. However, scanning technology lags far behind. Reading salt-stored data requires laborious electron-sweeping to decode each granular binary sequence–barely reaching megabytes per hour. However with time and resources, researchers are confident of unlocking faster optical reading methods. If so, humankind may achieve

Chapter 16

Tracing the Origins of Sea Salt Around the World

Its crystalline grains may appear identical, yet subtle qualities distinguish sea salt harvested regionally, a legacy of local climate, terrain, practices, and culture bestowing unique traits. France's fleur de sel, England's Maldon sea salt flakes, and Hawaiian pa'akai – beneath uniform white hides nuanced origins and stories connecting lands globally through a shared reliance on the fruits of the ocean, sun, and wind.

The most ancient, basic sea salt forms through natural cycles of tidal flow, concentrating aquatic minerals inland into shallow salt marshes and pans. As intense sunlight evaporates surface moisture, sodium chloride crystallizes for easy gathering once waters recede seasonally. This solar salt harvest persists in today's arid, low-lying coastal zones as it has for millennia, though often augmented by artificial evaporation ponds and pumps, accelerating yield. Yet when produced using traditional tools like rakes and wooden paddles minimally processed without anti-caking agents, solar sea salt manifests the concentrated yet balanced mineral profile distinguishing living seas rather than factories.

From subtropical islands like Cyprus to Mediterranean France, artisanal sea saltmakers pride themselves on preserving cultural traditions passed down through generations. Cypriots around Larnaca Bay still tend to shallow, stone-lined pans established by the

Roman salt trade, carefully timing harvests to ensure optimum texture and balanced nutrients like magnesium, which are critical to health yet easily destroyed by over-processing. Across the Mediterranean, Guérande's paludiers (salt farmers) roam the same black-bottomed clay marshes lining France's Atlantic coast, tilled by Celtic tribes trading this 'white gold' over two millennia ago. Raking the thin layer crystallizing atop these waters by hand at precisely the right moment, paludiers collect the region's prized fleur de sel ('flower of salt'), distinguished by signature large, irregular flakes that are delicately crunchy yet quick to dissolve.

Similarly, England's artisanal festivals celebrating centuries of sea salt legacy persist at boutique harvest sites like Essex's Maldon Crystal Salt and Cornwall's Halen Môn, using heritage methods unique to local climes and customs. Japanese seabed clay from the Seto Inland Sea also imparts a rich mineral balance and delicate sakura blossom aroma to sun-dried salts near Kyoto, still made using traditional bamboo evaporating boxes and hand-turned paddle wheels. This diversity of regional sea salts and harvesting styles highlights how even basic sodium chloride derives subtle yet distinct flavors from local environmental conditions—what the French call terroir.

Beyond Europe, solar sea salt production spans traditional palm-frond barns dotting America's Atlantic coast from Maine down to Florida, where colonial settlers boiled seawater as an early commercial industry. Pacific islands like Hawaii and the Philippines not only engage in long-standing harvest practices but also deep cultural connections bind communities through labor-shared harvesting in the saline-rich waters of fishponds and seabeds. Cleanliness akin to purification rites precedes Hawaiian families gathering each spring to harvest pa'akai, the glistening 'salt of life' blessing food and spirit. Similarly, Osonson pink salt crystals from the Philippines derive a delicate red tint from pristine clay beds saturated with iron oxide, magnesium, calcium, and potassium, where indigenous harvest rituals persist.

The unique mineral balance and flavors distinguishing solar sea salts are why artisanal harvesters increasingly highlight regional traits as valued hallmarks while innovating production to respond to the modern demand for specialty varieties. Yet whether packaged as trendy Himalayan or Peruvian pink salts or prized specialty flakes from France, what endures across ancient and modern sea salt appreciation is the connection through a shared dependence linking land to ocean, sun to sweat, and past to future.

Chapter 17

Himalayan and Andean Salt: Myths and Mountains

Towering peaks swaddled eternally in ice conjure images of remote mysticism and adventure for lowland dwellers, yet for indigenous mountain cultures, the soaring highlands prove home, spiritual center, and steadfast provider. While oxygen thins and cold intensifies upslope, mountains nourish life through precious minerals washed down from geologic uplift, the icy trickles aggregating to mighty rivers' that sculpt civilizations across Eurasia and the Americas. Among these rich deposits, veins of salt bestow mountains with mythic properties as geological phenomena, traded commodities, and health commodities across millennia, linking early trade routes through modern times.

The most otherworldly saltscapes spread below peaks soaring above the oxygen line, sterile badlands where only the hardiest survive. Such extremes forged northern Pakistan's Himalayan salt ranges: crushed seabeds vaulted skyward, then glaciated repeatedly over epochs, leaving scattered pinkish salt massifs. At 1700 meters up the Jhelum Valley's southern flanks, ten-story cliffs of crystalline halite from primordial oceans twinkle amid barren shale and gypsum, an improbable vision luring caravan traders spellbound by purity and abundance. Here in the 'Salt Range' city mechanism, local tribes both quarried dense salt to sell abroad by the tonne and hand-chiseled it for household use into intricate blocks embossed with Koranic verse or Mughal seal. Export-carved bricks traveled widely via Silk Roads and rail to forcibly add dietary iodine to British India's army and rural poor. At the same time, explorers like Alexander the Great's raiding forces returned awestruck accounts westward, extolling magical mountains "bearing salt as white as snow."

Equally, storied salt-bearing peaks pierced clouds above South America's oldest settlements, where the primal creator god Viracocha was said to weep salty tears seeding salt flats when struck by lightning, according to the Gede, Canas, and Paruro peoples near Cuzco. Sacred licks carved by wildlife moving downslope since the Pleistocene concentrated salt artesian upwellings dissolving subsurface deposits, drawing native Andean herds for essential mineral intake while hunters harvested meat and hides. Local tribes eventually began mining these concentrated subsurface brines circulating at Salinas Grandes, trapped by inland drainage radiating from the snow-capped Andes. Underground springs were diverted via aqueduct into thousands of ingeniously engineered solar evaporation ponds spanning the arid altiplano from Chile to Peru to Argentina—the largest industrial complexes of their era, circa 300 BCE. These ponds produced crops not of maize or coca but of the mineral 'white gold', which was so precious that it was used decoratively in masonry and currency for exchange.

Commercial salt-trading along developing rail and road networks laid the foundations for the Incan empire centered in Cuzco, the continent's first true city, supplying vast populations living at breathless altitudes. Stringent salt rationing also bred discontent, periodically erupting in riots whenever supplies ran low, or rulers restricted common access. But while emperors and governments exercised control over mineral riches, traditional mountain communities continued small-batch solar production using time-tested gathering techniques still employed today by cooperatives producing artisanal finishing salts treasured by global chefs for their unique texture and balanced mineral balance lacking in mechanized commercial production.

Pink to gray to black, the spectrum of exotic seasoned salts scaling Andean peaks shares mineral richness leeched from mountains' depths, their subtle hues and flavors imbuing heritage. These elevated, extreme salt flats continue to challenge engineers to devise access and transport for expanding global industries, as they have for civilizations throughout history. Yet traditional families still patiently tend to shallow ponds passed down through generations, their artisan batches indivisible from landscape and culture concentrated through patient sun and wind.

Chapter 18

Italian Sea Salt: Flavor from the Mediterranean

The Sparkling Shores of Italy's Salt Production

Italy's stunning coastlines have given rise to salt production for millennia. As the warm Mediterranean waters lap upon rocks and sand, salt crystals emerge. Human hands have carefully harvested these precious flakes since before recorded history. The earliest sites of Italian sea salt cultivation date back to the Iron Age, with saltworks dotted along coasts from Sicily to Apulia.

The ancient Romans first industrialized Italian salt production. They built elaborate systems of channels and basins to capture seawater and accelerate evaporation. Prominent families owned huge swathes of shoreline where slaves labored. The final crystalline "white gold" not only seasoned Roman cuisine across the empire. It preserved meat, fish, and produce that fed soldiers and citizens from Hadrian's Wall to Alexandria. Salt was also essential in rituals, used as salary payments, and levied with taxes that filled state coffers.

As civilizations rose and fell, traditional salt-making continued along Italy's shores. Independent farmers produced modest harvests for local markets using heritage methods. Extended families worked together, patiently waiting as sunshine drew out sodium chloride in well-worn salt pans. The age-old rhythm of the seasons governed production. Spring tides refilled ponds with channeled seawater.

Summer heat began the slow concentration. Fall winds aided evaporation until winter rains halted the annual cycle.

Medieval Italian merchants traded this sun-dried sea salt through the Mediterranean and beyond to northern Europe. By the 13th century, Venice controlled a quarter of the Mediterranean salt trade. Their broad, shallow pans in the Po River Delta supplied the alchemical secret for preserving colorful dyed textiles and glazing pottery. Salt's value rivaled gold, helping Venice become a dominant force in the Renaissance era.

Further south, family-run sea salt harvesting continued unchanged for a millennium near Naples. Local lore claims of salt taxes by Spanish conquerors in the 15th century sparked public riots that united into the first Italian resistance. However, history shows taxation existed long before then. More likely, prolonged heavy rains flooded the salt pans, halting production and causing shortages.

As the Baroque age dawned, improving sailing technology and New World competition disrupted traditional sea salt makers. Industrialization arrived in 19th-century Italy, with steam pumping systems erected along shorelines. While output increased, small-scale salt farmers struggled to compete against mass commodity production. Italy's 20th-century wars and globalized food chains pushed artisanal harvesting towards extinction.

Unique Flavors from Terroir and Tradition
What sets Italian sea salt apart lies in distinct regional terroirs preserved through generations of artisanal production. Location matters greatly, influencing mineral content and flavors extracted from the sea. In addition, traditional hand harvesting and solar drying methods concentrate on those signature essences of place.

From Sicily's mild aromatics to Apulia's gentle bite, connoisseurs recognize and relish the diverse offerings of Italy's sea salt.

Sicily gifts one of Italy's most popular finishing salts from its western corner near Trapani. Whitish-gray crystals with a soft texture and bright mineral notes derive from the island's shallow salt ponds. Local legend claims the sun god Helios hotly pursued the sea nymph Clymene here after she spurned his affection. As her teardrops fell into the sea, they solidified into salt. Today, salt makers patiently tend the Ponds of Nubia from late April through the heat of August, awaiting the concentration destined by nature. Strict parameters govern the salt's classification, dictating traditional tools and techniques. These ensure Sicily's 'sale Marino di Trapani' offers a touch of magic from antiquity to elegantly finished dishes.

Traveling the boot of Italy up the western coast brings Bitter Venetian Salt, a sodium chloride flake with true depth of flavor. Its gray crystals often contain traces of clay that tint them a light tan, remnants of tidal shallows around the Laguna Veneta. Hands scrape hardened salt from evaporated basins in July and August. Before industrial pumping systems, families transferred seawater bucket-by-bucket into the small jewel-like pans to slowly reduce. Funneled into pinecone-shaped mounds to drain for a month, the salt absorbs subtle pine resin notes. A hint of bitterness comes from magnesium chloride in these crystallized vestiges of the Adriatic Sea. Either sprinkled directly or crushed to finish hearty meat or fish, this salt coaxes out the richness of the other ingredients.

The Conero Riviera cradles gently curved bays streaked by brisk winds, creating ideal conditions for solar salt making near Ancona on central Italy's eastern flank. Salters divide tidal pools into wide stepping-stone flats, guiding brine into progressively smaller concentrators. Strict natural reserve regulations forbid machinery or pipes from interfering with endangered migrating bird routes. Instead, Align Sea Salt relies solely on clean ocean air to strengthen shallow pools, continuing a 500-year tradition. Rarely exceeding 11% salinity, these delicate pyramid-shaped crystals offer a mild mineral quality. Their notes of Mediterranean foliage and fauna infuse foods with what locals call "the breath of the sea."

Italian Chefs Champion Sea Salt's Culinary Qualities
From sophisticated Michelin-starred kitchens to humble trattorias, Italian chefs prize regional sea salts to balance and elevate their cuisine. Texture and delicate flavors enhance dishes without overpowering them. In addition to finishing touches, some salts lend their essence during cooking, too. Beyond purity, what matters most is matching salt character to ingredients and techniques. Nuanced artisanal sea salt deserves thoughtful pairing, not careless sprinkling. This careful attention coaxes out food's innate qualities.

For example, sea fennel and marsh samphire thrive amidst Sicily's salt flats, lending herbal and grassy aspects to the local salt. Thus, Trapani sea salt beautifully accents similar bright greens or vegetable dishes through its harmonizing notes. Another chef recommends blending Sardinia's cherry-hued salt into sniff-worthy olive oils to sprinkle over grilled bread, allowing pleasure to linger. The salt even provides a perfect souvenir, infusing the island's sunny warmth into homemade foods through the long winter.

Meanwhile, Apulia's gently biting crystal strikes a perfect contrast, tossed with rich burrata cheese or sprinkled over sweet melon to balance sugary juiciness. Similarly, bitter Venetian salt wakes the tongue before the next bite of tender cichetti seafood skewers dipped in white wine. And Conero Riviera salt blended into whipped brandied cream lends airy dollops a whisper of trees on an empty, windswept beach in the bite of tiramisu.

Such artistry rests on Italy's long-standing sea salt wisdom, keeping heritage and environment center stage. Strict consortium guidelines honor local methods proven through centuries of pleasing palates. This prevents contamination or overly bitter saline twists from chemical variations. What crystallizes year after year offers a taste of place, coaxed skillfully from the sea. Professional Italian chefs champion such cultural connections through each perfect pinch.

Chapter 19

Celtic Salt: Ireland and France's Grey Treasure

Long before provisions crossed oceans in refrigerated cargo ships, food preservation posed an ever-urgent challenge, one addressed over millennia through salt. Drying, salting, and pickling let ancient communities stockpile sustenance from seasons of plenty to guard against lean times, enabling settlement and trade. Among the northern Celts lashed by stormy Atlantic coasts, mineral-rich sea salt became such a coveted mainstay they used it for barter and payment, giving us the word 'salary' derived from the Latin for salt. Gre sea salt from Celtic shores is still seasoning local fare and thus bears the layered history of a people shaped by the skillful exploitation of this geological gift.

The grey tint distinguishing Celtic sea salt stems from clay rich in minerals leeched from the region's igneous bedrock, peppered with precious metals and rare earth elements. Iron, magnesium, calcium, potassium, and other nutrients concentrated through underwater springs or Atlantic storms filter inland, saturating coastal marshes and inlets around Ireland and Britain's Cornwall. Here, generations of local families erected stone ramparts against tides, funneled brines into successively smaller evaporation ponds, and patiently harvested the nutritionally balanced NaCl crystallizing as waters retreated. Wood-fired ovens torrified residue to intensify flavor before coarsely grinding particles by hand using traditional tools like granite querns turned manually–methods still used for small batch artisanal production favoring texture and delicate crunch.

Through Rome's expansion across Celtic lands circa 50 BCE, salt usage evolved from drying fish and meats to curing hams and cheeses for shipment as luxury goods to urban markets abroad. Tactically situated around natural harbors, monasteries like Ireland's Bangor Abbey became salt production hubs, processing local brine while importing more exotic flavors such as Spanish paprika and peppers to manufacture early charcuterie treasures later known globally as Irish bacon. French Breton salted shipped grey offerings abroad from Guérande, utilizing tidal channels and windmills powering pumps through the late Middle Ages, their plunder cooperatives growing rich enough to warrant tax levies funding further land reclamation.

By the 19th century, the concentration of ownership into fewer saltworks saw smaller family operations struggle against industrialized production. Many abandoned heirloom practices, like harvesting by hand or utilizing wood fires to kiln and grind dried salt blocks. However, the artisanal Celtic salt resurgence has recently tapped heritage methods to play up nutritive quality and pond-to-package integrity lacking in factory-refined products. Whether flakes or blocks infused with native herbs and healthful clays or employing stone wheels, linen bags, and wooden barrels for processing. Boutique brands like Ireland's West Cork Sea Salt and France's Le Paludier Guérandais are distinguishing regionally specific, small-batch crystal production now celebrated from farm-to-table kitchens to natural food stores worldwide.

The boom in artisanal finishing salts highlighting terroir has illuminated the preservation of near-forgotten local skills and lore. Brittany's plaudits once more tramp the labyrinth of briny clay ponds, sustaining their livelihoods like generations before them. Scraping early morning's prized salt crystals by hand within hours of dawn before destructive UV rays and rain can damage texture and flavor. Resuming the following day and day after season upon season, the grey Celtic seas continue depositing their rich mineral harvest along storm-whipped shorelines as they have for millennia.

Chapter 20

Hawaiian Paʻakai: Island Salt Harvesting Traditions

The Hawaiian Islands rise from the azure waters of the Pacific as jewels borne of volcanoes, their black sand beaches, and jagged cliffs, belying a rich history spanning centuries. Alongside the land's fruits and the sea's bounties, one of the most prized commodities harvested in old Hawaiʻi was paʻakai, a natural sea salt cherished for its pure flavor and versatility.

For the Native Hawaiians, paʻakai was much more than just a seasoning. Believed to impart foods with the life force or mana of the sea, salt held an exalted status in Hawaiian culture and figured prominently in legends, rituals, and daily life on the islands. The knowledge and practice of making paʻakai were passed down from parents to children over countless generations, cementing salt's enduring legacy in Hawaiʻi.

The traditional Hawaiian method of salt-making exemplified balance with the environment and sustainable harvesting of natural resources. Families living near the ocean would collect seaweed, limu kohu, which grew abundantly on underwater reefs near the shore. Piling limu koha on racks built above tide pools and shallow flats, they would wait for days as sunlight evaporated the water, leaving behind glistening salt crystals, paʻakai pākai, treasured for its bright flavor.

Limu kohu was the seaweed of choice for Hawaiians to make quality pa'akai, as it contained the most natural salts and minerals while giving the finished salt its characteristic reddish tint. Besides seasoning food, red alae salt, tinted with volcanic clay, held ceremonial significance and was used to bless and purify spaces and newborn babies. The labor-intensive gathering and processing ensured that pa'akai was regarded as a sacred, precious resource in old Hawaiian culture.

The best sea salt was made during the summer, when trade winds blew steadily, and rainfall was scarce, enabling rapid evaporation. Elders carefully watched weather patterns, timing harvests according to the favorable seasons for salt production. They passed this indigenous knowledge on to the young, synchronizing culture and lifestyle with nature's rhythms. Salt harvested thus was considered infused with mana from the skies, sea, and salt-makers alike.

Kamā'āina families living by the ocean had their own carefully guarded salt-making sites passed down generations. The mostly flat, shallow pu'u pa'akai (salt flats) were surrounded by small stone walls, allowing seawater to fill basins. Various grades of salt resulted from this sun-drying method, depending on each family's technique. The most prized large coarse crystals formed a fine finishing salt called pa'akai 'alae, later commercialized as Hawaiian sea salt.

Besides weather and seasons, traditional Hawaiian salt-makers closely observed the phase of the moon to determine the best times for gathering limu kohu seaweed and evaporating seawater. Ku, Kane, and Lono were Hawaiian gods associated with fishing and farming, embodied within moon cycles. Salt harvested by their cosmic dance was deemed to be most infused with mana.

The semi-tropical Hawaiian climate, with alternating periods of rain and steady dry heat, made for ideal salt production. Extended droughts, however, posed a threat, as freshwater streams feeding irrigated inland crops could dry up without rain. Extended rainfall, on the other hand, hampered salt harvesting by diluting ocean pools. Through astute observation of weather patterns, kupuna (elders) balanced these cycles for optimal agriculture and aquaculture.

Children were included in the salt harvesting ritual to teach respect for nature and to stay in tune with the seasons. Young girls often gathered limu kohu, singing songs passed down generations while filling baskets with the ruffled red seaweed. Younger children helped pound dried salt crystals into finer powder using stone mortars and pile wood pestles. Older boys assisted elders in building and repairing rock walls, holding tidal pools, and developing skills passed down through oral traditions.

Hawaiians used salt as a multipurpose seasoning, preservative, ritual offering, and spiritual cleanser. Its cleansing and purifying properties formed the basis for the cultural practice of blessing newborn babies with salt. Midwives rubbed a pinch of pa'akai over a crying baby's skin, mainly under tiny fingernails and inside ears, to cleanse away remnants of the womb and welcome new life. Sprinkling a circle of salt around a new home was believed to bless and protect its inhabitants.

The redox balance of sodium and chloride made salt an effective meat and fish preservative before refrigeration existed on the islands. Hawaiians salted excess catch such as ulua (jackfish) and aku (bonito tuna) to store for later, allowing extended provision in case of poor fishing due to storms. Salt-cured fish and shellfish became delicious delicacies, added to stews or eaten by themselves. Salted meats accompanied vegetables like taro or sweet potato as sustenance for work parties, building fishponds, and irrigated terraces.

While cooking in earth ovens, Hawaiians used herbal sea salt seasoned with endemic herbs to flavor meat and fish. Ti leaf wrappings enveloped food with infused salt crystals, redolent of island terrain. The characteristic smoky aroma from kiawe or mango wood enhances the flavor of ancient Hawaiian cuisine, with herbal sea salt as the cornerstone seasoning, tying disparate ingredients into harmonious, satisfying repasts. Mahalo nui loa no ka pa'akai! (Thank you very much for the salt!)

Besides direct use as a food flavoring and preservation, Hawaiians also used salt to tan hides. After scraping the inner skins of small mammals like rats or birds with volcanic glass, rubbing them with sea salt and kinolau (bark ashes) helped convert raw pelts into durable leather. Salted and tanned furs had varied uses, such as decorative capes for alii (chiefs), protective coverings for drums, envelopes for sacred items, and even unique artwork.

Salt was so highly valued in old Hawaii as a precious commodity that it became used as monetary currency. When commoners offered thanks to Ali'i (royals), it was often in the form of gourds filled with pa'akai. The 6 to 10-inch dried gourds, called ipu pa'akai, were intricately decorated with dye made from kukui nut ash.

 Chiefs would commission master gourd carvers to fashion elaborate containers to store and transport salt procured as tax from commoners. Pa'akai ipu was also gifted during Makahiki, the ancient festival celebrating Lono, god of agriculture and fertility, to encourage future bountiful harvests of all island crops, including salt.

So highly prized was it that grades of pa'akai were designated as superior ritual offerings. The highest priest, Kahuna, received coarse pa'akai 'alae blessed under a full moon. Lesser priests got fine pa'akai, while commoners offered gourds filled with mundane salt crystals for blessings. The exalted status of Hawaiian solar-evaporated sea salt across social strata exemplified its sacred mana-infused nature.

All inhabitants of old Hawaii respected the life spirit embodied in pa'akai, understanding it came from Papahānaumoku, the Earth Mother goddess who gave birth to islands from union with Wakea Sky Father god. Ancient chants equated pristine pa 'akai with new-fallen snow atop frigid Mauna Kea, treasured as a sacred gift from deities. Just as sweet water streams gave life-sustaining water on land, glistening crystals rising from briny tidal pools gifted health and joy when respectfully gathered.

Hawaiians traditionally used summer's heat to produce solar-evaporated sea salt, saving cooler months for agricultural crops benefiting from rains. This demonstrated interdependent harmony between the land and sea realms, following natural cycles for mutual prosperity. The collapse of robust indigenous aquaculture and agriculture following Western contact underscores the consequences when this sacred balance was disrupted after 1778.

In mere decades after British explorer Captain Cook first landed on Kauai island in 1778, introducing Hawai'i to the outside world, native culture, already suffering from influenza and measles, was further ravaged by the breakdown of time-tested systems after the establishment of the Mamalahoa Trail across Big Island allowed foreign disease and pests to invade pristine valleys, destroying harmonious cyclical agriculture patterns disrupted by invasive ungulates like goats and cattle.

Previously isolated natives lacking immunity rapidly succumbed to waves of smallpox, typhoid, influenza, and even the common cold, decimating the population across all islands over the ensuing decades. Estimates suggest that 90% of pure Hawaiians perished from introduced diseases by the mid-1800s. With death tolls mounting and social structures shaken, traditional salt-making was one of many customary practices pushed toward extinction.

The unregulated exploitation of sandalwood forests above ancient irrigated terraces generated quick fortunes for Western traders while bringing erosion and heartbreak to Hawaiians watching their watershed conservation efforts collapse. Despite the trading rights of the Kamehameha king to license sandalwood harvests, shortsighted overlogging denuded watershed forests. With it faded sustainable prosperity from old Hawai'i's well-regulated agriculture, aquaculture, and renewable forestry.

After sandalwood forests were stripped, whaling ships found a haven in Hawaiian ports for fresh food and water. While they brought trade opportunities, their crews also introduced deadly epidemics and voracious appetites. By the 1840s, the Hawaiian monarch was forced to lift ancient kapu taboos to protect people's health and natural resources to ensure basic survival. The cultural system in a delicate equilibrium, sustaining native islanders for centuries, lay shattered alongside dreams of sovereignty.

From 1820, American Christian missionaries flocked to Hawaii, hellbent on converting souls even while inadvertently destroying their bodies through imported disease. Condemning Hawaiian spirituality and ceremonies as devilish, they banned sacred hula dances critical for passing oral wisdom. Incantations celebrating the rainbow goddess Kapoina'I were suddenly silenced while generations of priestly lines abruptly severed. Banning the use of pa'akai in blessings and rituals struck at the very heart of Hawaiian identity.

Outlawing native customs and beliefs to replace them with foreign religion may have reflected good intentions. Still, it ended up depriving proud people already traumatized by apocalyptic depopulation of their only solace. Adding cultural assault to biological ruin essentially torpedoed the canoe. Bereaved Hawaiians secretly clung to their rich oral heritage, even while bowing heads to Sunday sermons and hymns for the new Western deity Jesus.

While missionaries blamed native religions for societal collapse, the truth was more complex. Unchecked introduced diseases coupled with uncontrolled Western immigration and business pursuits threw old Hawaii's delicately balanced ecosystems and governing structures into unsurvivable chaos for inhabitants completely unprepared for such rapid change. Blaming victims and banning customs integral to their cultural identity added a grievous insult to already devastating injuries.

With death tolls mounting astronomically from one new imported disease after another, traditional Hawaiian society strained beyond capacity, simply trying to perform sacred burial rituals central to spiritual beliefs, while mourning elders dying faster than their wisdom could be passed down. Protecting natural resources like forests through disciplined conservation practices of old already buckled under pressure to feed crowds of whaling crews.
Watching sandalwood forests groaning ancient chants as they fell to British trader's axes proved too much for proud Hawaiians already watching their future bleed out on missionary clinic cots strewn with kinsmen's blackened corpses decaying faster than their despairing families could bury them. Under the incomprehensible

tragedy of the apocalyptic scale, the orderly world sustained through humble rhythms passed down generations evaporated as quickly as shallow pools shimmering with sacred salt.

Amidst such desperation, arriving opportunists sought to capitalize on the leadership void left as revered Ali'i perished without successors surviving. By the mid-1800s, missionaries conspired with treasonous ali'i and merchants to overthrow the Hawaiian monarchy, justifying it as the divine will to civilize heathens. Queen Lili'uokalani was deposed by the self-righteous coup plotting missionaries' children, who proclaimed a republic and then had her arrested in the beloved Iolani Palace.

Thus, the sovereign kingdom lasting nearly two millennia, even through waves of warriors from Tahiti and bloody battles between rival chiefs, could not withstand the arguing Christian fanatics who toppled the rightful queen before granting themselves private ownership of all crown lands whose sacred trusteeship Lili'uokalani fought vainly to defend on behalf of her dying race. Betrayed to the last by capitalist-bearing troops to enforce their right to rule and plunder paradise.

From less than 200 foreigners in 1820, the population swelled to over sixty thousand by the 1890s, vastly outnumbering the remaining pure-blooded Hawaiians. The native culture was reduced to entertainment for tourists even while the Kingdom of Hawaii was relieved of governance by conspiring missionaries. Sacred pa'akai gathering sites were trampled by crowds of foreigners building resorts and homes atop ancient heiau temples once tended by kāhuna high priests.

Hawaiians became outcasts in their homeland, forbidden to speak their native language in new American schools established to indoctrinate remaining youth into Christian beliefs and Western lifestyles. Forbidden previously to swim in pools reserved for Ali'I, remaining natives were now restricted from their shores in favor of hotels charging hefty tourist rates. Jim Crow attitudes relegated Hawaiians to subservient roles, serving wealthy foreigners and privileged new landowners, mostly descended from opportunistic missionaries.

Rich in minerals from millennia of volcanic eruptions and blessed by a bountiful climate, the Hawaiian Islands once sustained a vibrant civilization for over fifteen hundred years. They traded sustainably with other Polynesian cultures while nurturing a religion glorifying myriad nature gods primordial to the Pacific, governed by sacred Ali'i priest-kings and queens ruling through divine mandate. Their cyclic lifestyle in harmony with land and sea was disrupted when Captain Cook's 1778 arrival opened the floodgates to ruthless foreign exploitation.

Once proud keepers of an earthly paradise where pristine nature was worshipped and safeguarded as the embodiment of potent gods, remaining Hawaiians by the start of the 20th century found themselves condemned as little more than inconvenient remnants in an All-American vacation resort. Their spiritual world shattered alongside their ecosystems, robbed of sovereignty in their homeland, haunted by ghosts of elders keening laments for all that was lost. The bitter taste of disenfranchisement replaced the once-sweet crystalline tang of sacred solar-evaporated sea salt.

From the 1970s, a cultural renaissance brought renewed pride in Polynesian heritage to younger generations of Native Hawaiians. Reviving indigenous arts, sports, and language helped strengthen the identity of a people struggling with some of America's highest rates of poverty, incarceration, and suicide after a century-long assault on their ancestral island kingdom. Protecting remaining tracts of pristine coastline and rainforest watersheds turned into a sovereignty struggle.

Renewed interest in recovering disappearing cultural practices such as traditional salt-making sparked a small revival. But gathering natural sea salt today is prohibitive for most Native families without rights to shorelines dominated by mega-resorts. Some community-based nonprofits holding small parcels of shoreline have restarted teaching Hawaiian youth the ancient arts of gathering seaweed to process sun-dried salt, which is much harder to practice now with so few families possessing ancestral salt flats passed down generations.

In modern Hawaii, indigenous pa'akai, once gathered freely by Native Islanders, is now a premium gourmet commodity targeted mostly for upscale tourism markets, making its labor-intensive harvesting challenging to sustain. The sacred mana, once infused by prayers while gathering limu seaweed and solar-drying briny crystals, is a shortcut using mechanized evaporation. While retaining mineral content from volcanic soils and untainted Pacific seawater, the cultural context anchoring its deep-rooted significance is diminished.

Yet glimmers of hope remain with some Hawaiian families who are still stewards of historic pa'akai sites, continuing generational traditions of producing supreme salt using venerable methods. Pristine shorelines survive untouched by hotels in a few remote districts controlled by Native Hawaiians, preserving vital ecosystems still abundant with endemic seaweeds and rare nesting sea turtles. The youth here learn ancient arts guided by impassioned elders committed to perpetuating a nearly lost salt-making heritage once woven into everyday island existence.

The periodic crumbling and collapse of Kīlauea volcano periodically spreading new fingertips into the sea symbolizes how Pele goddess still grows Hawaiian islands even today, her fiery power undimmed. Winds and waves patiently smoothing new peninsulas into glistening ebony sand shores demonstrate the ever-shifting nature of creation. In sweet water streams trickling to nourish once arid lava flows or spewing geysers hissing primordial secrets from deep within Earth's molten heart, profound mysteries still nurture those who respectfully listen, promising to reveal newly emerging facets gleaming with ancient wisdom, like iridescent paʻakai glistening shyly through sunlit shallows glowing turquoise with boundless promise.

The enduring allure of paʻakai harvested using ancestral Hawaiian methods boils down to profound layers of accumulated mana passed down generations who chanted prayers to gods while gathering limu seaweed and watching it transmute into gilded sun-dried salt. Infused with spiritual potency from a culture living sustainably in harmony with their island ecosystem for over a thousand years through cyclical rhythms, genuine Hawaiian sea salt retains a rich heritage linking the past to future generations.

Sharing a communal bowl of poi with kin to the tune of slack key guitar, graced by a light sprinkle of paʻakai still made using long-tested ways, thus offers a symbolic chance to savor sacred linkage to storied ancestors who likewise feasted on fruits of the ʻāina (land). One glittering salty crystal suffused with oli spirit chants conveys a deep reverence for the bounty of land and sea realms that sustained Native islanders physically and spiritually before Western contact forever altered the islands' fate through disease and conquest.

In old times, humble Kalo farmers and fishermen gifted their chiefs pa'akai out of duty. Today's salt-makers donate proceeds to groups that protect indigenous rights and fragile island habitats, still nourishing Native families as they have for generations. More than just flavoring food, modern pa'akai offers hope of reclaiming a stolen heritage and building bridges of unity to heal bitter divisions. From the ancient island past to the destitute present, this sacred gift of salt seeks to enrich the collective future.

The enduring cultural significance of pa'akai across centuries in Hawai'i reminds us that often, what nourishes the body through flavor also feeds and anchors the soul. Salt forms essence, evoking identity, place, ancestors, and pivotal stories.

The collapse of the sovereign Hawaiian kingdom resulting from unchecked foreign capitalist interests and diseases, coupled with bans on native religion and cultural practices by overzealous American missionaries, no doubt exacted a devastating loss for the dignity and livelihoods of Native islanders watching helplessly as their homelands were stolen from underneath generations who sustained a thriving civilization in balanced harmony with the natural bounties of land and sea. However, the islands have proven resilient thanks to the enduring mana (life spirit) passed down by ancestorial guardians who are still active through geographic features, creating new land even today.

Ancient Hawaiians derived profound meaning from natural cycles like Pele's continuous expansion of islands through lava flows, seeing divine signatures in Earth's creative destruction. They found reassuring renewal in lapping waves patiently smoothing fresh black sand shores into established coves, sheltering rare green sea turtles before new coconut groves sprouted to offer nourishing fruit. Constant regeneration visible across various ecosystems held deeper promise that the cycles of justice will eventually return dignity and self-determination to those dispossessed of their homeland.

Indeed, the 1970s Hawaiian Renaissance, introducing aspects of lost culture to younger generations, sparked renewed pride in Polynesian identity that strengthened community bonds, providing vital social support networks previously fractured by historical trauma. Rediscovering heritage arts like hula dances, long-distance canoe voyages tracing ancient migration routes, and revitalizing endangered languages helped alleviate the despair plaguing many Native families struggling with soul wounds inflicted by generations of colonization. Reclaiming cultural practices offered pathways to reconnect with ancestral roots, providing stability and purpose.

Gathering to pound tapa cloth or pluck melodies from slack-key guitars built solidarity, while sharing oral histories brought cathartic healing unaddressed when the pain was muted. The humble pa'akai crystal once again graced community tables as families remembered old ways of gathering limu kohu seaweed from local shorelines, then sun-drying it on pu'u racks into shimmering salt containing the mana of elders now revered rather than silenced. Younger Hawaiians found hope in reclaiming their own identity on their terms.

For many Native youths alienated from churches run by outsiders, demeaning their spiritual beliefs, learning rituals used by their great-grandparents, which honored gods embodied in local landforms and wildlife, allowed them to reconnect with native religion on a deeper level. Respectfully gathering herbs growing near volcanoes brought them closer to understanding Pele, the volcano goddess, as a living protective force rather than mere superstition. Watching salted fish and seaweed dry on racks under gently swaying palms while listening to soothing chants sung by grandmothers kept ancestral wisdom flowing to nourish young minds.

Chapter 21

Japanese Salt: Pure Flavor from the Seto Inland Sea

Framed by Honshu, Shikoku, and Kyushu islands, the Seto Inland Sea offers one of Japan's most scenic vistas: over 700 tiny islets scattered amid vibrant coral and cerulean waters, the whole panorama framed by mountains gently rising behind. Yet this tranquil seascape bustles with oyster farms and historic harbors testifying to the sea's bounty, including a precious crystallized harvest dating back millennia: salt from the sea and sun-dried amid these protected tidal pools using age-old techniques running generations deep.

The unique climate, terrain, and practices responsible for this region's salt can be traced to geography, both isolating yet sheltering these midland waters from Pacific storms. Encircled from the open ocean by Honshu's mountainous spine, over 300 days of annual sunshine concentrate brine pumped from local aquifers into a sprawling patchwork of man-made evaporation ponds hand-tended by salt farmers called Senshi. Sun-warmed, mineral-rich waters percolating bedrock and primordial seabeds amass over three years of reduction into increasing dense brines, which enshi carefully divert for final collection into wooden drying boxes called tama-bashi. Here, solar heat and breeze finish evaporation atop bamboo mats, crystallizing delicate pyramid-shaped flakes raked carefully to avoid minute iron contamination from metal tools.

After careful hand-drying, sorting, and packaging, the result is shio: pure white salt crystals delicate as snowflakes, prized for enhancing savory umami foods like sashimi and tempura due to perfectly balanced sodium and minerals absorbed from the sunlit sea.

Salt production developed early around the Seto Inland Sea, merging practical livelihood and cultural customs for coastal villagers. By the Asuka Period (~500-700 CE), during the adoption of Chinese administrative structures and Buddhism, state treasuries and temples financed salterns, providing precious mineral revenue. At the same time, local enshi became hereditary salt-making families and tended sites passed down generations. Careful timing of harvests using moon phases and tidal charts maximized yields from salt farms relying on the balance between the sea, earth, and human effort in a mutually sustaining relationship. Regional varieties also emerged using local clay filtration beds to derive signature textures and flavors, from delicate Sakura cherry blossom to robust red Umboshi salt.

Over a thousand years old yet still in operation today, Ako City's Tekaki Saltern offers the world's last surviving wood-burning salt production, employing traditional techniques predating industrialization. Visitors touring the carefully preserved salt huts observe enshi maneuvering each painstaking step essentially unchanged from the Edo era when such salterns provided sodium desperately needed to supplement rice-centric diets among peasants and samurai alike.
Tekaki's rich dark grains still draw celebrity chefs and specialty grocers, valuing handmade craftsmanship signifying purity and balanced nutrition refined through patient sun, sea, and fire alone—without bleach or additives plaguing mass-market refined salts today.

From the serene sea and labor carried through generations emerges this singular salt-distilling Japanese aesthetic reverence for nature through human effort. The devoted enshi, artfully bending to task rather than seeking to dominate their environment, thus practice craft as meditative discipline aiming toward perfection through simple daily rituals aligned to seasonal change. Their briny harvest connects past and future in delicate crystals subtly saturated with culture and care unique to each place.

Chapter 22

African Salt: A Pinch with a Past

A substance once literally worth its weight in gold, salt illuminated and indirectly named the continent it helped transform over millennia. Ancient trade caravans trekking southward in search of fabled salt mines believed to lie amidst dark, uncharted lands named their destination accordingly: Bilad al Sudan meant 'Land of the Blacks' in Arabic, later truncated in European tongues simply to Sudan or Africa. Yet salt's influence in opening the interior through early long-distance trade also indelibly flavored regional cuisine, celebrating this essential mineral's heritage spanning empires, innovation, and hardship.

The first great African salt trade arose in the Sahara Desert, where precious 'white gold' concentrated in subterranean veins or solar evaporated from paleolithic lakes drew Moor, Arab, and European merchants southward despite harsh conditions to supply their salt-starved homelands. Goods exchanged for this essential preservative were found to be used across the Sahel in salt-poor regions, such as gold, ivory, spices, and slaves. Timbuktu's storied rise as an influential medieval trade hub and seat of Islamic erudition owed everything to its prime access near Mali's northern salt mines, the lifeblood of regional commerce by the 14th century, when Ibn Battuta described it the finest destination "on the face of the earth."

Yet the mineral's imprint stretched deeper over the continent than the explorer's trails. Dried and salted fish became dietary staples extending inland from abundant Atlantic and Indian ocean coastlines. At the same time, native desert cultures like Namibia's Herero augmented scarce grazing with salt gathered painstakingly from Etosha pan each dry season, preserving milk and meat against the long voyage returning to ancestral highland plateaus. Brine springs bubbled up amid the Great Rift Valley Concentrated through Maasai solar ponds, providing precious minerals for both herds and tribes-people while influencing unique cultural customs around oral history and hospitality.

Eventually, direct control and intensive taxation of mineral rights across European colonies bred conflict and unrest, with Gandhi's famous defiance foreshadowing independence struggles and winning self-determination after centuries of exploitation. Yet salt's enduring legacy survived through cuisine linking coastal tribes with inland farmers and herders through traded ingredients like Mchuzi wa Samaki: rich Nile perch stewed with leafy greens, cassava, and coconut milk spiked with grey sun-dried sea salt flakes or dark pink gatherings from the distant volcano-fed Lake Katwe. Diffused southward by Bantu tongues, the word connecting diverse cultures across vast terrain derives from the proto-word *tùu for native salts crystallizing along endless shorelines and pans leading to uncharted interior realms once known only as the "Land of Salt."

Today, from the Red Sea coral coasts to the grey-white Makgadikgadi flats of Botswana, artisanal salt makers Africa-wide honor timeworn gathering or evaporation practices, producing finishing salts displaying a spectrum nearly as diverse as the land and people themselves. Somali women along the Horn still use wooden rakes to glean crystallized red and orange chunks from saline mangroves lining the coastline near Berbera. These solar sea salts balance the iron and iodine missing from bland refined table salt, adding delicate flavor and crunch to spicy stews or roasted meats. The Afar people of Ethiopia carry on seasonal salt harvesting and transport by camel caravan from the blistering Danakil Depression 100 meters below sea level, just as their ancestors did when camel trains supplied ancient Aksumite emperors and Egyptian pharaohs over three millennia ago. Their broad, flat golden slabs derive minerals leaching deep underground from geothermal springs, lending a subtle sulfuric, iron-rich taste relished on meats from another region's timeless trade.

www.ingramcontent.com/pod-product-compliance
Lightning Source LLC
LaVergne TN
LVHW041318200726
843509LV00009B/542